The Gulf Within

The Gulf Within

Canadian Arabs, Racism, and the Gulf War

Zuhair Kashmeri

James Lorimer & Company, Publishers
Toronto, 1991

Canadian Cataloguing in Publication Data

Kashmeri, Zuhair
  The gulf within

ISBN 1-55028-347-2 (bound) ISBN 1-55028-345-6 (pbk.)

1. Iraq-Kuwait Crisis, 1990-1991 - Arab Canadians.* 2. Arabs - Canada - Social conditions. 3. Arab Canadians - Social conditions.* 4. Muslims - Canada - Social conditions. 5. Racism - Canada. 6. Canada - Race relations. I. Title.

FC106.A65K3 1991   956.704'3'089927071
F1035.A7K3 1991 C91-095320-1

Photo section: Zuhair Kashmeri

James Lorimer & Company, Publishers
Egerton Ryerson Memorial Building
35 Britain Sreet
Toronto, Ontario
M5A 1R7

Printed and bound in Canada

DEDICATION

To the Arabs and Muslims of Canada, in the hope that they unite and advance the struggle of Canada's visible minorities; and

To my uncle, the late Professor A. A. A. Fyzee, a scholar *par excellence* of Islamic and Middle Eastern studies, whose following words began my unceasing love affair with Arabs and the Middle East:

> I would invite my friends to go into the burning sands and be stunned by them; to see the dawn in the Syrian desert and the sun rising above the Nile, silhouetting the Mohamed Aly Mosque in Cairo; a little later to hear the call to prayer in the myriad-voiced radio or at the Ummayyad Mosque at Damascus; then to enter a suk and drink black coffee in the tower of Babel or Fishawy; thence to do business and pay five liras for what was worth one and be fooled ... and laugh at oneself; then to eat kebab and have a fertile discussion ... about philosophy, law, politics, as unreal and devoid of practical wisdom as the doctrine of Maya....

CONTENTS

PREFACE

"Arab Canadians had no evidence to justify their allegations of harassment by Canadian security agents during the war in the Persian Gulf ... the complaints were probably motivated by a 'private agenda' or a desire for publicity."

John Bassett, chairman of the Security Intelligence Review Committee, as quoted in the *Globe and Mail*

T he seeds of this book were sown over coffee in the cafeteria of the *Globe and Mail* in Toronto. My partner in that emotional conversation was Rick Groen, one of the finest literary writers at the paper. It was the first week of the Gulf War, and we had agonized over headlines such as "Allies Bomb Baghdad" and television footage from the glass-eye of an American missile streaking towards its Iraqi target. But there was clearly something missing in all this cheering and jingoistic coverage — the Arab-Muslim viewpoint, the Arab-Muslim culture — it was almost as if that entire population had been dehumanized.

There were stories quoting Iraqi President Saddam Hussein saying that the soldiers of the U.S. coalition would "swim in a sea of blood," a graphic metaphor when translated verbatim from the Arabic into English, but as common as "kick his ass" in our vernacular. Rick wanted me to get involved in the war coverage, which, given the territorial workings of the *Globe*, was not possible. He went on to write four brilliant commentaries in the Arts and Entertainment section of the paper, focusing on the TV coverage. After all, this was a living room war, but the depth of coverage was not sufficient to "float goldfish."

As the one-sided bombing progressed and Canadians were caught up in the euphoria of this Nintendo war, another missing element became glaringly apparent: What about Canadian Arabs and Muslims? They were human, they were right here, and they were the enemy by extrapolation. I decided to call Aida Graff, former Dean of Women at Victoria College, the University of Toronto and a leading Canadian-Arab spokesperson. "It is madness," she told me on the telephone. "It's terrible. I just heard of an Arab boy, nine or ten, who was kicked out of his classroom for disputing that Hussein was a Hitler." Elias Hazineh, a Palestinian from Mississauga, Ontario, told me about an Arab dentist who had been crossing the border into Buffalo, New York, for months, doing a large-scale research project for an American company. Like clockwork, after January 16, his Canadian citizenship became worthless, and he was extensively fingerprinted and photographed by American authorities at the border. In Hamilton, Ontario, a white woman was refused service at a supermarket because she wore a scarf that resembled the Muslim headdress, or hejab. An Iraqi Canadian in Toronto was hounded by the Canadian Security Intelligence Service because their bugs had shown his telephone traffic was up. CSIS wondered if he was planning an act of terrorism in Canada. In fact, the media wanted to speak to a real, live Iraqi Canadian, and the Canadian Arab Federation had given reporters his telephone number. The Royal Canadian Mounted Police, meanwhile, were knocking on Arab doors without warrants.

If all these actions did not amount to persecution and harassment, then the two words need to be redefined. And where were the knights in shining armour — the media — in all of this? To borrow an analogy from Rick Groen, the coverage was like the "quickie book" published after a major event. It "provides a service to the more patient historian down the road, less for what it contains than for what it leaves out — in that sense, it neatly reflects the prevailing mood and assumptions of the moment."

This book, then, is not about the Gulf War but about the racism and the harassment experienced by Canadian Arabs and Muslims as a result of Canada's decision to participate in it.

This is also a book about a country, Canada, which claimed high moral ground in the world and promised to show other nations how different nationalities and cultures could live peacefully under one roof. After giving the world multiculturalism for decades, Ottawa under the Tories unleashed its security forces against Canada's Arabs and Muslims.

And if I had any doubts whether the substance of this book deserved a permanent place before government historians paint the era with the brush of tranquillity, it was dispelled by a lunch conversation with Howard Bernstein, an award-winning TV producer and my guru and mentor in the world of radio journalism. After listening to some of my findings, Howard's jaw dropped, and he said, "How in the hell did the media miss all of this?"

How indeed?

Zuhair Kashmeri,
Toronto, June 21, 1991

ACKNOWLEDGEMENTS

I would like to thank James Kafieh, Randa Fares, Mary and Khalid Muammar, and Ibrahim Hayani of the Canadian Arab Federation in Toronto, Bill Luand in Montreal, and Sami Araji in Vancouver; Aida and James Graff and Andrew Van Velzen of the Near East Cultural and Education Foundation; Rashad Saleh and Elias Hazineh of the Canada-Palestine Association; members of the Canadian Arab Society of London; Asif Javed and others of the Society for Islamic Unity in Montreal; Abdullah Massih Thomas, head of the Canadian Chaldean Association; Khalid Iqbal of the Manitoba Islamic Association; Professor Harish Jain of McMaster University; Rick Cash of the *Globe and Mail* library; Beth Davies of the University of Toronto; the office of New Democratic Party member of Parliament Svend Robinson; David Jacobs; Jasbir Singh of the World Sikh Organization's Edmonton chapter; Khan Rahi, director of the Metro Toronto Social Planning Council's Action Access Council; Multiculturalism Canada; my brother Sarwar Kashmeri of New York; and scores of other Arabs and Muslims too numerous to list.

In the preparation of the manuscript, special thanks go to Gail Lem for reading over my book proposal; James Lorimer for taking less than thirty minutes to realize there was a book in my faxed proposal; Diane Young, his tireless editor for her support, and Lisa Betel, his Toronto fix-it-all, for her unceasing help and cheer; Helene St. Jacques, for reading and commenting on the first three draft chapters, Andrew Van Velzen, for doing the same with my conclusion; the Ontario Arts Council and the Department of Multiculturalism and Citizenship for research and writing grants.

A special thanks goes to Said Zafar, imam and international trade consultant, for advice and help too abundant to detail.

Last but not the least, I want to thank my wife Gulrukh, son Shamil and daughter Shireen, and Ole Gjerstad, an honorary Kashmeri, for help, guidance, and for playing surrogate dad to Shamil and Shireen while I undertook this project.

INTRODUCTION

"Leaders make policies; the people pay the price."

Professor Saleem Qureshi, University of Alberta, Edmonton

For most Canadians, the Gulf War was a distant experience, viewed through network cameras and the hurried news reports of scores of Western reporters. But for some Canadians, the war was neither distant nor evening entertainment.

These were Canada's Arabs and Muslims. The Canadian Arab Federation estimates that there are approximately 250,000 Arabs in Canada, about 200,000 of them followers of Islam. In addition, Canada is home to at least another 100,000 Muslims from places as diverse as Guyana, Fiji, India, Pakistan, Africa, Eastern Europe, the Soviet Union, Malaysia, and Indonesia.

For most of these people, the devastation wreaked by the U.S. bombing of Iraq meant either a missing relative or friend, or the destruction of a familiar neighbourhood. Or it meant the mass killing of fellow Muslims or Arabs. And the country they had adopted, Canada, was party to this destruction and slaughter.

The Gulf War also meant that a segment of the population came under suspicion — Canadian Arabs and Muslims. Those who had the most to mourn were also suspected of subversion; they were questioned by the security forces and subjected, in some cases, to instances of intolerance, racial harassment, and violence.

It did not matter that thousands of these people were second-, third-, and fourth-generation Canadians. The community felt that it was under siege.

This, then, is the backdrop to the stories recounted in the pages that follow, a re-creation through oral histories of the experiences of Arabs and Muslims during the Gulf War. Although the book focuses on a relatively small number of families and individuals between Montreal and Vancouver, the incidents and emotions are fairly representative of what the community faced across the country during the tumultuous period of the war. In fact, the main characters in this drama were chosen after I had talked to more than seventy Arabs and Muslims across Canada, during and immediately after the war. The seventy came from varied backgrounds: a linen-supply truck driver in London, Ontario; an economist in Montreal; a convenience store owner in Mississauga; a religious leader in Edmonton. Included are non-Arab Muslims. Many of the men have the same common names — Mohammed and Hussein — and many of the women wear the traditional hejab. Like the rest, they too became the enemy within. The reason for these extensive interviews was to determine whether some of the troubling stories that I had first heard were being repeated across the country. I discovered that they were.

The book proceeds geographically, beginning in Edmonton and moving east to Montreal. But geography takes second place to the individuals and institutions explored through the tales. Hence, the story of Imam Youssef Chebli of Edmonton is also the story of the city's media in particular and the institution of the media in general. In a similar fashion, the tales explore political parties, city government, the police, CSIS, the educational system, crown corporations, and the mental health system, all against a backdrop of multiculturalism. The book ends with an examination of the role of the national security forces, the media, and multiculturalism during the war.

The chapters retain a structure that was impressed on me during the interviews. I was fascinated by the backgrounds of the individuals, by their stories of the old country, by the rigours of settling in a new land. Some of this material is included towards the beginning of the chapters in order to do something that our media did not — provide a human dimension. By telling the stories of individual Arabs and Muslims, I hope that readers can forget about skin colour and religion and empathize with their plight. There but for the grace of God, go I.

Since I am a reporter, I decided to organize my material using my instinct for news gathering, coupled with a feel for the ethnic sensitivities that lay behind the narrative. Where it moves away from conventional journalism is in its attempt to give readers a historical perspective — something that our mainstream media and their obsession with today's events have neglected.

For many readers who continue to believe that the Gulf War was fought on distant shores, this book will come as a surprise. The establishment media did not cover this side of the war. But it happened — and it left a scar that will take years to heal.

Part I

CHAPTER ONE

The Media Imam

"An untamed tongue can be as full of deadly consequences as any warhead."

Bonnie Gustafson, in a letter to the Edmonton *Sun*

As the first American bombs dropped on Baghdad with laser-guided precision on the evening of January 16, 1991, the same scene swept through hundreds of newsrooms across Canada. Front pages were ripped apart to accommodate the beginning of the Gulf War, headlines were bloated to huge type sizes, and thousands of computer terminals were plugged into the incoming news services to follow the action. But by the next day there was a new question for journalists to answer: How do we bring this war home to Canadians? That local angle must exist somewhere in this vast land. Sure, there were the families of the armed forces personnel in the Gulf, but they had been milked dry even before the war started. And, of course, there were the evening television shots of Canada's CF-18 jets taking off on escort missions and then returning to their bases, the pilots saying how they felt left out while their American, British, and French counterparts were levelling Iraq. Then there was whispered talk of Islamic and Arab terrorism in Canada — good copy, but ambiguous. Weren't there any local villains?

It was in this mood that an enterprising reporter in Edmonton decided to call up a good-natured and garrulous Muslim leader. The idea was to provide local copy by soliciting the views of Imam Youssef Chebli. What Chebli told the reporter proved beyond his wildest hopes. Not only did the imam not agree with

Canada's involvement in the war, but he also appeared actively to support Saddam Hussein. The local angle was getting better — a villain at home is worth two in the faraway killing fields.

Chebli's story became a war within a war. He was like a child suddenly put under the glare of spotlights; he loved it — after all, it was his chance to expound the contrary Islamic viewpoint. As he responded to the media, they would quote the portions of his statements that fit their agenda. Chebli stirred up a controversy that put Canadian Arabs and Muslims on the defensive, turned Canada's foreign policy on its head, and sent the security forces scrambling to determine whether Alberta's Muslims were about to stage a Rielesque rebellion on the Prairies. The repercussions were deadly for everyone around Chebli. But Chebli's tale, like any good one, has a beginning and a middle, a human face absent from the headlines he attracted.

Youssef Chebli was one of eight children of a Lebanese land-owner-farmer in the fertile Bekaa Valley. The family could afford a comfortable lifestyle and education for the children. Chebli himself wanted to enter the medical profession and had his career mapped out when, in keeping with the volatile and sudden twists that continue to shape the destiny of the Middle East, his life was changed. A cousin he greatly admired, a rich businessman in Brazil, called on the family one day and told Chebli that he must become an imam, a religious scholar and prayer leader, and spread the word of Prophet Mohammed — the messenger of Allah. Chebli dropped his plans to become a doctor and headed to Cairo's ancient, world-famous Al-Azhar University. When he graduated in religious studies from the faculty of languages in 1968, he was assigned to the most fertile oil patch in Saudi Arabia — Dammam.

Canada's own oil patch was far from his mind in Saudi Arabia, where he met the likes of Sheikh Bin Baz, the Khomeini of that Calvinistic Muslim land. Reportedly, Baz still believes that the world is square and that a human who walks to its edge will fall off. But Chebli believed Allah had mapped out a bigger job for him than minding the flock in the Prophet's birthplace. He had to carry the word to a non-Muslim country.

He followed the path trod by the first Arab immigrants to Canada, those who came here in the late 1880s and early 1900s.

Edmonton seemed a good location. Hadn't the Chebli clan started settling there before the First World War? He remembers the day he left Dammam in 1970 — it was stifling; the temperature reaching 100 degrees F during the day. Less than twenty-four hours later, at three in the morning, he landed at Edmonton International Airport. It was the middle of winter, and the temperature was 35 below.

It was blistering cold, he said, remembering how he shivered as he disembarked from the aircraft. Outside, his family waited to receive their newest member. He recalled gazing outside the airport at the blanket of snow and uttering his first words in Canada: "I'm not going out there on that white stuff. Are you crazy?"

Less than two years later he was the imam, or religious leader, of Edmonton's Grand Mosque, the Al-Rashid. The original Al-Rashid was Canada's first mosque. The state of affairs that Chebli first encountered in Edmonton's Muslim Ummah, or community, reminded him of the mosque's early history when there were only about twenty Muslim families in Edmonton. One day in 1938, they decided that they needed a place of worship where their children could be taught the faith. Using contributions from Christian Arabs and other locals who were enthusiastic about the idea of a mosque in that largely British city, they obtained a building permit and erected a one-storey structure.

"When I came here, maybe twenty or thirty people would come and pray, sometimes two or three," he said. "Not like today." A week earlier, more than two thousand believers crammed the new Al-Rashid Mosque for the mandatory Friday prayers. That was on a Good Friday, a statutory Christian holiday when Muslims can fulfil the Koranic injunction without having to appeal to the sense of fairness of their bosses to get the afternoon off. The usual Friday attendance, though, is still about one thousand.

Surrounded by a modern subdivision, the new Al-Rashid Mosque displays the traditional dome and minaret. The old structure was replaced in the early 1980s with the help of a generous $1-million grant from Libya. The older mosque, meanwhile, was removed to a site at Fort Edmonton Park, purportedly as a historic monument among other artefacts of the city's early days. Although local Muslims proudly point to this gesture, city authorities appear to have paid little attention to it — the mosque's presence in the park remains unmentioned in a colourful brochure Edmonton publishes to attract tourists.

Both Canada and the mosque were good to Chebli. He and his wife Maria — a half-Lebanese, half-Spanish woman with large, black eyes — settled into a condominium rowhouse in Castle Downs, a neighbourhood with a large ethnic population in the city's north end. Their family grew as two Canadian-born daughters were added to the two sons who had come with them. They acquired cars and televisions and video recorders and kitchen gadgets, and soon Chebli was certified by the Alberta School of Theology as a registered minister.

None of the $1-million-dollar grant from Libya found its way into Chebli's basement office, which lacks the trappings of most church offices with their ornate wooden desks and chairs. Its simplicity, however, is in keeping with the thirteen-hundred-year-old faith that now embraces almost a quarter of humanity in its fold, about one billion people. A large metal desk is the major piece of furniture. On the wall next to it is a calendar from Mecca. It features the holy Kaaba, a cube-shaped building surrounded by a sea of humanity — Muslims on pilgrimage, fulfilling one of the five pillars of Islam. Glued to the wall on the other side of the room is the Canadian Charter of Rights and Freedoms.

Outside the office it is another story. Screaming little girls and boys run helter-skelter along corridors that are decorated with the pictures that children draw in primary schools — portraits of their mothers with big eyes and hair-raising hairdos, scenes from the playing field with an oversized sun. They are the students of Edmonton's only Islamic school, which teaches the required provincial curriculum in a Muslim setting.

Chebli's workload at the mosque is a far cry from the quiet life led by imams in his old country. In his own words, a Canadian imam is also "a counsellor, teacher, soldier, hospital man, court man, and immigration man." In one day, he might deal with cases as diverse as those of a Kenyan woman who is beside herself because she has lost the receipt for a graveyard plot next to her husband and of a Palestinian refugee seeking to transfer his claim from Ottawa to Edmonton. Stroking his grey beard and straightening his flowing long black robe, Chebli said that a Canadian imam was the equal of a thousand imams in the Middle East. They pray five times a day, lead the Friday prayers, give their sermons, and go home.

But Chebli took all this additional work in his stride, much as he had accepted the snow and the blistering cold. What continues to bother him, though, is the acute crisis that he believes North American society has slipped into. Twenty-one years after his arrival, his mission was not yet accomplished. On the one hand, there were the offspring of believers, trapped like one of his sons by material temptations. They needed a lot of guidance. On the other hand, there were non-believers, who also needed to be told about the message of Islam, the faith that had swept the globe from Asia to Europe within the first hundred years of its founding.

"Islam is a universal message, and we don't have to hide it for ourselves; we have to deliver it to the whole world, and if we don't, there is severe punishment," he said. "If my neighbours are Christians, Jewish, or whatever, if they don't hear my message, on the day of judgement, they will defeat me. They will say: 'God, he was sitting beside me, we were smelling the same air, drinking the same water, under the same sky, and he never opened his mouth to give me the message. O Allah, don't blame me, blame him.' And I will get the blame, and He will object to my going to heaven."

The one constant in the life of Chebli has remained Islam. It was Islam that led him to support Muslim Iran during the eight-year Iran-Iraq war that ended in 1988. His rationale was that Iraq, a predominantly Muslim country, had violated religious edict by invading another Muslim country that was in the midst of setting up the first Islamic nation in centuries. And his Friday sermons then attacked the policy of Iraqi President Saddam Hussein.

It was Islam that inspired him to continue galvanizing support for the Palestinians as they were pushed off their land and scattered all over the world into a diaspora, much like what the Jews had experienced for centuries. He supported Libya's strongman, Muammar Gadaffi, as a Muslim revolutionary, even as the West billed him as a terrorist. And it was Islam that instantly caused him to stand up and support Iraq against the U.S.-led coalition.

As the clock ticked towards the American-inspired United Nations' deadline of January 15 for Iraq to remove its troops from Kuwait, the neighbouring country it had invaded on August 2, 1990, Chebli decided to pay his first visit to Baghdad, to attend a world Islamic conference. It was January 7, and the mood was tense in the Iraqi capital as President Saddam Hussein continued to defy "the forces of imperialism led by the United States." Chebli was in the company of two other Canadian imams from Ottawa and Montreal.

Chebli's visit was not appreciated by the few diplomats Ottawa had left behind in Baghdad as it lined up its meagre forces behind the U.S.-led coalition. According to intelligence sources close to External Affairs, one of the diplomats even attempted to find out the contents of Chebli's remarks at the gathering by trying to coax an Iraqi into co-operating with him. The Iraqi instead informed the country's Mukhabarat, or secret service, of the overture.

Chebli's position at the conference, he said, was very clear. He opposed Ottawa's decision to join the coalition and wage war against Iraq. The coalition, he told those attending the conference to thundering applause, was "the work of Satan, a satanic coalition." He believes that Canada's trademark the world over is its peacekeeping forces. "That upset me to see our image demolished [by] the position of our government. I was caring as a Canadian, and I love to see people calling us … peaceful people; that is why I was fighting and opposing the position of our federal government. … I felt we were not an independent country. … I felt we became an [alter] ego to the United States. … We [Muslims and Arabs] did not expect Canada to send jet fighters to kill our mothers and fathers."

He embraced the coalition's arch-enemy, Saddam Hussein, and kissed him on both cheeks, a traditional Arab greeting that is as common as shaking hands in the West. He endorsed a resolution stating that Hussein was indeed the new Caliph of Islam because he had brought the plight of the Palestinians in the diaspora centre-stage with his brave acts. And he endorsed Hussein's Jihad, an Arabic word that simply means struggle but that is persistently and very loosely translated by the Western media as a Holy War. The struggle that Chebli was endorsing, however, was the cause of the Palestinians and the right of Hussein to stand up to Washington rather than bow down and acknowledge its supremacy. He never endorsed the invasion or takeover of Kuwait. On January 15, the day before hundreds of U.S. planes rained bombs on Baghdad with more power than the nuclear weapons unleashed on Hiroshima, Chebli left for neighbouring Jordan.

Back in Edmonton, the *Journal,* the tabloid *Sun,* and the broadcast media were scrambling to get reactions from local Arabs,
especially Iraqis. One of the reporters called Chebli's home, and
twenty-six-year-old Mohammed Chebli answered the call. "Call
my father. He's in Jordan, and he'll tell you what is really happening," the eldest son said. He gave the reporter his father's
telephone number in Amman.

When the media called, Chebli reiterated his warm meeting
with Saddam, his endorsement of the Jihad against a satanic coalition murdering Muslims and Chaldean Christians in Iraq, and his
total opposition to Ottawa's policies. When the Edmonton *Journal*
spoke to him in Amman, the imam gave the reporter what he felt
were the facts and stated what he believed in. The *Journal* ran a
story headlined: "Local Muslim Cleric Sees Saddam as God's
Agent."

"What I spoke was the truth, [but] the media flamed the statement and showed their true colours. They said, 'You are
supporting Saddam.' And I said: 'Yes, I am supporting his cause,
his cause is not Kuwait, [it is] the Palestinian problem. This is the
mother of all problems. If you don't solve it, the war between Iraq
and the allies is the beginning, not the end.' ... I told them, in
Islam if any Muslim country is attacked, Muslims must stand up
and defend it as one; otherwise, you don't belong to the Ummah,
the nation of Islam. ... I said it [the coalition] is a satanic movement; it is madness. The big sacrifice to the world is truth, and
the big win, hypocrisy."

What he was saying was not very different from what a lot of
scholars and other commentators worldwide had been saying
without using the Koranic or Biblical idioms. Stephen Lewis,
former Canadian ambassador to the United Nations, accused the
United States of hijacking the U.N. Security Council to get its
stamp of approval for an unjust war. Archbishop Michael Peers,
primate of the Anglican Church of Canada, declared that the
coalition's reasons for starting the bombing did not meet the
Christian tests for a just war. Noam Chomsky of the Massa-
chusetts Institute of Technology said the U.S. army had become
the world's "rent-a-thugs," renting itself out to the Kuwaitis for
billions of dollars in subsequent rebuilding contracts. Why then
highlight Chebli? Every mosque has an imam who leads the
prayers and offers advice on religious matters. Unlike the Chris-

tian church, Islam has no hierarchy. A Muslim is directly responsible to his maker. An imam cannot claim to represent the
views of the entire community, and Chebli never did. Spotlighting
him was like questioning any Muslim on any downtown city street
and running with a story that said, "Muslims Back Iraq."

For the reporter and his editors, Chebli was a wonderful figure
on whom to peg a story. Focusing on him, they could dramatize
the war by quoting an Edmonton imam who backed a government
that was being compared to Germany's and a leader who was
being compared by the authorities to Hitler. With Stephen Lewis
or Michael Peers, criticism of the war effort raised questions about
the Canadian government's policies. With Youssef Chebli, they
had a source who could be presented not as a respected Canadian
religious leader, but as a local advocate of the war policies of Iraqi
leader Saddam Hussein. And that was exactly how the Edmonton
Sun and many other media outlets played the story.

January 18 is etched in the memory of Maria Chebli. It was
about 9 A.M. when the telephone rang. "Can I speak to Mr.
Shelli," said a voice at the other end. She replied that no such
person lived there, that this was the Chebli residence, and that Mr.
Chebli was away. She politely asked the caller to leave a message.
The response was a volley of obscenities, and she hung up the
phone. Every second minute, it seemed, the phone rang. Other
callers cursed everything from Islam to her Arab heritage. One
caller said: "You bloody Muslim, go back to your bloody
country." She replied: "My bloody country is Spain, my bloody
country is Lebanon, and my bloody country is Canada." She said
she felt embarrassed saying this because she feels Canada is her
true home, since she has spent most of her life here. Eventually she
told the caller that she was probably a better Canadian than he was.

Maria finally called the police. She said that on the first day
after her husband's interview was published, she received more
than a hundred hate calls. They continued for the next three days
as the police tried to trace the callers. Involving the authorities,
though, had its own drawbacks. Maria was forced to listen for at
least a few minutes so that the calls could be traced. But she
always found it impossible to do so and would end up slamming
down the receiver.

On January 21, the source of her anguish returned to Edmonton
secretly — Chebli had instructed his family not to tell the media

or any of their friends about his arrival. But, in Maria's words, her husband could not zip his lip and stay away from politics. And each time she ended up "in the middle." Having started the ball rolling, the media were hungry for more. The Edmonton *Sun* interviewed Chebli on January 22, and on page five the next day, the tabloid ran a short interview with a headline that read: "Muslim Backs 'Hero' Saddam." The story repeated his earlier remarks. And the telephone began ringing off the hook again.

The first caller that morning began his conversation by swearing. Maria recounts their exchange: "I said, 'Excuse me, can I help you?' He said, 'You and your family will be dead in ten minutes.' I said, 'Oh my God, I am lucky, I have at least ten minutes.' " The man began to swear again and she hung up too soon for the call to be traced.

After the fifth caller had threatened to blow up the Chebli home and machine-gun the children, Maria panicked and kept both doors locked. Anybody who showed up was asked from the inside what his business was. She angrily told her husband that he was a sheikh — another word for imam — and as such should not make political statements. When he protested that the media were distorting his words, she asked him to avoid reporters. But Chebli's zeal to tell the world about Islam increased with each caller.

Meanwhile, Maria's patience had begun to wear thin. She is a freelance Spanish and Arabic translator in the local court. Although she wears the hejab, a scarf, at all times in keeping with her husband's religious feelings, her desire for peace of mind was gaining the upper hand over her oath of loyalty to Chebli. Hence, when a man approached her in court one day and asked her whether she knew the controversial Chebli, since she bore the same last name, she decided she had had enough. "There are more than a hundred families who are Chebli; that means I have to be like Chebli?" she replied, disclaiming any connection with the controversial imam. She told Chebli later that she was not ashamed of him but did not need any more headaches.

As Maria described the ordeal that forced her to deny their relationship, Chebli stared at his briefcase. He did not want to get involved again in a discussion that had already occurred numerous times in that tumultuous period. Later, in the absence of Maria, he would once again be a lion — his name comes from the Arabic *chebl* or lion's cub — and say with a flourish, "There is no place in this world for cowards." But within earshot of Maria, he was silent.

January 24 brought a new dimension to the Chebli saga. Mohammed received a call from his twenty-one-year-old brother, who was at the coliseum watching a hockey game. Nazir was with an older friend, who suddenly asked him whether he would fight for Canada "over where you come from." Nazir replied that if Canada was attacked, he would fight for Canada. "But what about what your father said," the friend asked. The son said his father had the right to say what he wanted and, besides, "they rearranged his words in the paper." Unconvinced and angry at Nazir's support of his father's statements, the man suddenly punched him and threatened more. Nazir called Mohammed, and soon five Arabs armed with hockey sticks faced ten whites armed with pool cues across the coliseum. The whites were hurling insults like "You crazy Arabs, you crazy fuckin' Iraqis, we'll teach you how to be Canadian." In the melée, Nazir was hit and broke a bone above his left wrist. Finally, Maria and Chebli intervened and called the police, who charged the man who had initiated the incident.

The next day, a reporter showed up at the mosque at prayer time and wanted to talk about the war and politics. Three believers had to restrain Mohammed Chebli from physically ejecting the reporter. He screamed: "Get out or pray, politics outside, now we pray for peace. Leave the mosque." Mohammed was convinced that the torture his family was living through was the handiwork of a biased media. A few hours earlier, when there were just a handful of elderly Muslims at the mosque, a former soldier had shown up on the front steps and screamed: "Where is that Chebli? I am going to kill him. I was in the army, and I am going to teach him a lesson."

The harassment continued. Every day at the mosque, Chebli freely discussed the hate calls he was receiving, but he hid the mail from his parishioners. He ignored the hate mail, he said, because he did not want to unleash a torrent of retaliation from local Muslims. It was hate mail at its worst. One letter read: "You Fuckin 2-faced Moslim Traitor see what will happen to you and your family soon. There will be a bloodbath of you'll cowardly, hypocritical, ungrateful Moslim Pigs, Bastards and Mother-Fuckers in this country — ISLAM the corrupt, hypocrits, cowards, thieves and ungrateful PIGS religion — you will be dead soon."

Another writer had clipped photographs to create a collage. At the bottom was a picture of Saddam Hussein with a big smile on his face. Saddam's face was turned slightly to the left, almost touching the exposed penis of a white man whose picture had been clipped and pasted to tower over that of Saddam. A label next to the white man's picture read, "GOD." "This, my dear brother, is Western civilization," said Chebli, holding the letter in one hand and the collage in the other.

But Chebli's troubles did not end with hate calls and hate mail. The media attention raised questions in Ottawa, in the war cabinet. And the agencies who were put on the spot over his outburst were the Canadian Security Intelligence Service and the Royal Canadian Mounted Police. Ottawa wanted to know whether this one-man rebellion in Alberta was the beginning of a Muslim revolt.

Unlike several other Arabs, who were asked to report to CSIS offices, in Chebli's case operatives met him in his basement office at the Al-Rashid Mosque and sat across from him on his own sanctified turf. Two officers showed up on Monday, January 27. Chebli was dressed in his full regalia, the black robe and long white imam's turban, with his beard combed neatly. They wanted to determine whether his call to Muslims to support their brethren could mean that the believers would rise up in rebellion in Canada.

Chebli said he had had enough of his words being "rearranged" by the media. And so he decided to tape the two-hour interview. He would not be outdone by the Canadian Mukhabarat. During the interview the exasperated Chebli said he threatened to throw his Canadian citizenship card at the officers, asking them to rip it up along with the Charter of Rights that was pasted on his office wall. He told the agents that Canadian Arabs were peace-loving people but that the government did not differentiate between right and wrong, that it copied President Bush and his demands. He attacked the government for targeting Arabs simply because they were recent immigrants and pointedly asked the two about their heritage: one was Irish and the other Ukrainian.

Chebli recounts: "They said, 'We don't want to see violence in Canada,' and I said, 'Who invites violence? You, yourself. We [Arabs] have a clean history here in Canada, but you [incite] us to make violence. ... I tell you, if you want violence, we are prepared, we have courage, we are not cowards. How many professors, doctors, psychiatrists [have you consulted] and still you have not been able to understand the mentality of Muslims. When you understand, you will make peace. ...' "

Chebli also told the officers that he could "turn Canada upside down" if he liked by encouraging Muslims to rise up against Canada's involvement in the war, but he would not because he was an imam, a leader, and meant to provide a good example to others to guide them on the right path and encourage tolerance, patience, respect, and understanding.

Chebli's boasting, coupled with his idiosyncratic pattern of speech, was a gift to a villain-hungry media. But the essence of his message to CSIS was that instead of questioning his loyalty, they should team up with the RCMP and find the people who had terrorized his family and scores of others in the community. His remarks came after almost two weeks of harassment. Undoubtedly, the agents kept in mind his other activities in the community, such as his involvement with Christians and Jews in the interfaith council. They were more straightforward and understanding in their reporting than the media. The vivid Arabic images that Chebli translated into English, a hyperbole not uncommon under stress for people whose mother tongue is not English, had to be discounted by about 80 per cent. The report they filed said the possibility of any terrorism emanating from the Al-Rashid Mosque was zero.

Later, CSIS Director Reid Morden told the editorial board of the Edmonton *Journal* that he would have preferred that Chebli not express his views when tensions were running high in Canada, but that his men reported that Chebli "was not a fulcrum that was going to lead to downtown Edmonton being in flames." Given the mood of Edmontonians after the news reports, CSIS might have had the good sense to issue such a statement through the solicitor general to cool off the tension. It never did.

Instead, CSIS reports, in those wartime days, were circulated to other agencies, such as the Royal Canadian Mounted Police and Customs. And not everyone believed the assessments. Chebli began noticing a black van parked outside his house every day. He believed that it was an RCMP surveillance vehicle. He was under the gun, and he knew that his mail was being opened. A magazine he had been sent from a friend in Amman, with write-ups of his Baghdad trip, was seized by Canada Customs and held for four days until Customs determined that the articles in it were unlikely to incite Canadian Arabs to terrorism. He was notified about the seizure.

As the Chebli controversy grew to national stature — he was soon featured on shows such as the Canadian Broadcasting Corporation's national radio show "As It Happens" — voices of dissent were heard among the Muslims. The RCMP and CSIS had questioned other Muslims about Chebli — subtly forcing them to distance themselves from their religious leader. The media lent the security forces a hand here by helping to split the community. After first building up their straw imam, reporters began questioning other prominent Muslims about Chebli's statements as reported by them. Their questions were usually rhetorical. Largely out of fear for their families and their children, individual Muslims began dissociating themselves publicly from Chebli's support for Saddam Hussein and the Islamic cause. "His job is just to pray and teach religion. He doesn't carry any influence," one local Arab told the *Journal,* adding that Chebli had no influence that would encourage the community to rise up in violence.

The committee that runs the mosque itself decided that it was time to muzzle Chebli, since the media continued to besiege the mosque. Mohammed (Mickey) Jomha, president of the Canadian Islamic Centre, which runs the Al-Rashid Mosque, had earlier issued a statement saying that Chebli was speaking for himself. Jomha and Larry Shaben, a former minister of housing and industries in the Tory government of Peter Lougheed, now decided on even more proactive measures. The two decided that Chebli should refer all media requests for interviews to Shaben, and Chebli gave in. The media were not enthusiastic about having to deal with Shaben; he was too much like them. Yes, they could say that he was a Muslim, an Arab, but he was part of the establishment in Alberta and hardly likely to stir up a heated controversy.

Shaben laughed as he described the disappointment of the media over the Islamic Centre's decision to move Chebli off centre-stage. "So when the reporters came later, and they were trying to get Chebli to say something, they would be told: 'You have to talk to Larry Shaben.' And they did not want to talk to me. It was really fascinating in the last month or so because it's no fun talking to Larry Shaben. They wanted to talk to somebody who'd say: 'Hey, Saddam is okay!' "

Not only did the media avoid Shaben at this juncture, but they also refused to give him the same profile as Chebli during the war, despite his prominence. Shaben traces his ancestry to Lebanon. He had expressed his views in a number of public meetings; he said that Canada's Gulf posture was all wrong and that Ottawa should never have joined the war. "Look at the way the West functioned with the Soviet Union," he told one audience. "Seventy-three years we waited to deal with the Russian bear and five months with a tiny Middle East country." He said it was clear Canada's foreign policy was driven by the United States. Canada neither needed Arab oil nor was it motivated by a high moral conduct; otherwise, it would have taken similar steps when Israel invaded Lebanon in 1982 and killed thirty thousand people, when it annexed Syria's Golan Heights, and when U.N. resolutions asked Israel to withdraw from occupied Palestinian territory. None of Shaben's comments drew much press. But then Shaben was dressed in a suit and tie, he had never projected himself as a Muslim in his political career, and his speech used imagery that fitted the mould of the establishment. Besides, he was not a garrulous imam, the former minister's loyalty could not be questioned, and he could not be caricatured.

There also was another dimension, which Chebli's son hit upon in his down-to-earth manner. By seeking out dissenters who could be typified as Arabs and Muslims and not simply as dissenting Canadians, the media had set up the community for a fall.

The journalists' motives in spotlighting Chebli were to find controversy and drama, not to provide balanced coverage. They depicted him as an archetypal villain and left the impression that he had tried to incite Canadian Arabs and Muslims to commit acts of terrorism, which he had not. Had the reporters asked Chebli whether he had endorsed Saddam Hussein's human rights abuses in Iraq or the war with Iran, he would have said no. He was simply commending Hussein for challenging an imperialist power and bringing the Palestinian problem to the world's attention. He did not even support the invasion of Kuwait; he simply felt that the two Muslim countries could have resolved their problems without interference from a Western armada.

No one disputes that it is the responsibility of the media to reproduce the spoken words of a person accurately, but reporters need to exercise common sense when their subjects are not fluent in English. Reporters who are determined to emphasize an angle have an advantage over interview subjects struggling with words. They can ask leading questions or quote selectively, giving the interview a slant the subject never intended.

But the most important duty of a journalist is to provide context and balance in any story. Chebli's stand on the Gulf War was only a few notches stronger than that of Canada's mainstream Christian churches. Most churches believed that the Gulf War was not just. Had the reporters wanted to cover Chebli fairly, they could have included the views of the other three imams in Edmonton and of well-known Muslim leaders in the community.

But how exciting and sensational would a story be if it said: "Muslim and Christian Leaders Oppose Gulf War?" And how exciting would a story be if the other imams and Muslim leaders opposed the American-inspired war but did not support Saddam Hussein as Chebli did, which would imply that most Muslims were no different than Canada's pacifists? Balance and context don't always produce dramatic and saleable journalism.

And Chebli was a yarn that could be respun a hundred times and still produce headlines to sell papers.

CHAPTER TWO

The Token Arab

"Hopefully it won't come to this, but if you and your family ever need a sanctuary, come to our house to hide."

A white Edmonton mother's offer to her Arab neighbours

Riad Majeed is a fixture in Edmonton's Grand Mosque, the Al-Rashid. In addition to his striking appearance — overweight, a round face and sharp eyes peering from behind his glasses — Muslims at the mosque remember him as one who ambles slowly, weighs each word carefully before he speaks, and smiles a lot. "Alhamd-ul-illah," or praise be to God, is his usual response when someone throws the traditional Canadian greeting his way: "How are ya?"

But there is something else that he is known for in Edmonton's Arab and Muslim community — his loyalty to the Progressive Conservative Party of Prime Minister Brian Mulroney. If he is a fixture in the mosque, he is equally a fixture in the local Tory party, which, in his eyes, symbolizes Canada's future and can do no wrong.

As an ethnic, Majeed is unusual: he threw in his lot with a party that is generally considered right wing and white dominated. But the party was good to Majeed. And the universe unfolded for him the way he envisioned. If other ethnic Canadians were suffering at the hands of their white compatriots, there was something wrong with their attitude, or maybe their politics. He could not understand many of their complaints, and some of the ethnic groups say he avoided them at times for fear of antagonizing his party.

It was hardly surprising then that when Majeed's universe came crashing down around him during the Gulf conflict, he was astonished. He was puzzled that his own loyalty was questioned and that his community was the subject of right-wing fury. But his puzzlement soon turned into anger, and he went into a period of self-questioning, his earlier self now in a frozen posture and the new Majeed, very conscious of his Iraqi background, pondering his past and his future.

Majeed is an engineer by profession. He came to Canada from Iraq in 1973 with his Lebanese-born wife. Their two sons, Kemal, fourteen, and Basil (Mike), ten, and six-year-old daughter, Salma, were all born in this country. Majeed is well-educated, typical of the elite — enterprising and outgoing. He had no problems finding jobs in Canada and no problem finding his way around the political structure. There were two things that brought him to Canada. One was to better his own standard of living. The other was his image of Canada as a peacekeeper and its boast that it would be the first country where nationalities from all over would live together peacefully. Like thousands of other Arabs, he had been impressed by the policies of Canada's peacekeeping forces in Cyprus, in his own region, and in Israel right after the Suez crisis in the 1950s. Here was a white nation that, while a member of the Western military alliance, was at least showing some semblance of impartiality. He was pleasantly surprised to see that Canadians came in all shapes and colours, and over the course of time he did develop a special liking for the country and its multicultural reality.

The Majeed family is Muslim. At home the children are taught about their parents' religion and culture, both Iraqi and Lebanese. The family prays regularly at the Al-Rashid Mosque, fasts during the thirty days of Ramadan, and makes sure that it joins other Muslims in Edmonton in celebrating special feasts. Watching the Majeeds break their Ramadan fast at sunset with two hundred other believers in the basement of the mosque reveals the true spirit of multiculturalism — an equal level of comfort in both the dominant and minority cultures.

But outside of this milieu, the children are brought up all-Canadian. They are encouraged to play Canadian sports like hockey and to get involved in school and community activities. Often on their summer holidays, rather than return to Iraq for visits, Majeed would take them to different Canadian provinces so that they got a good feel for the geography and culture of their homeland. Kemal, in fact, received a certificate from the governor general for participating in sports and community activities. He was one of five children from Western Canada to receive this award. The passion with which Majeed talks about Canada is unusual from a first-generation Canadian.

When he decided to join the Tories, he gave the party the same kind of commitment. In fact, when you step into Majeed's living room, it is like walking into a miniature museum of the Progressive Conservative Party. There are Tory emblems and memorabilia everywhere. High up on the book shelf is a black swivel base with eleven little rods protruding from it. Each has a different flag, one for each of the ten provinces and a Maple Leaf. It is an artefact that is only found in the offices of cabinet ministers, says Majeed proudly, adding that he gained one for his loyalty to Canada. Then there are the photographs of Majeed, his chubby, spectacled face peering out between Prime Minister Mulroney and "a well-known national columnist" or standing with External Affairs Minister Joe Clark, the mayor of Edmonton, the premier of Alberta, and other bigwigs. But his most prized possession is Brian Mulroney's tie — a tie that he took off and gave to Majeed. "Would you believe it," said Majeed, "he gave me his own tie."

Some of Edmonton's Arabs call him a Tory flunky, the ethnic face that the party loves to flaunt everywhere to back its claim that it has the interest of Canada's minorities at heart. But Majeed is very serious about his role as Tory. He sees himself differently, as a loyal Canadian who believes that the Conservatives are the best thing that could have happened to Canada. He had used his connections with those in power to help his community — the Iraqis and the other Muslims in Edmonton, playing Mr. Fix-it when his help was sought and when it was politically expedient to do so.

Being a Tory loyalist and an ethnic has its rewards. Majeed was appointed to a government refugee committee and, in return, agreed to serve on several other committees, including those of the mayor and the premier. And he always swore publicly that he did not believe that there was discrimination in Canada under the Tories, that by and large this country treated its visible minorities very well.

He continued displaying this optimism even as the Iraq-Kuwait conflict began heating up in early 1990. Majeed was confident that because Arabs like himself had held audiences with people in high places, their input would be asked for and taken into account when the Tories shaped their foreign policy response to the impending crisis. Surely the Tories knew that there were several generations of minorities who had been attracted to Canada because of its image as peacemaker. He and the other Iraqis expected Canada to take a neutral stand. It might condemn the invasion of Kuwait, but beyond that it would distance itself from the aims of Washington.

And so, when the Iraqi army marched into Kuwait and Canada joined the other Western countries at the United Nations in condemning the invasion, the response was acceptable to Majeed. After all, no politician could support an invasion. But then, Majeed began noticing a worrying trend as his friends in Ottawa veered towards a policy that copied that of the United States. Washington was responding with troops and ships, supposedly to protect Saudi Arabia, in an operation called Desert Shield. Its ships were mounting a blockade around Majeed's old country. And Canada was actually committing ships to join its ally on the grounds that it was a United Nations' action. Majeed found it strange that the Liberals and New Democrats were the ones raising objections and cautions, and not the Tories. And he could not dismiss the fact that the decision to send three Canadian ships was made by Mulroney.

This decision was the first jolt for Majeed. He and other local Iraqis had been meeting regularly to discuss the Gulf. The initial consensus among them was that they did not believe the Western media's story that Iraq had invaded Kuwait. They believed that Iraq was invited in by Kuwaitis who had staged a coup seeking to dethrone the emir. Iraq made this argument after the invasion, but its version never got the headlines that George Bush's or Brian Mulroney's pronouncements got. The problem was how to get the Iraqi version of events across to the Canadian population before it was totally brainwashed. Majeed soon took steps that put him at odds with his political masters.

One morning, his telephone rang. It was a reporter from an Edmonton paper who was seeking the reaction of local Iraqis to the crisis in the Gulf and Canada's involvement. This was the first of several interviews Majeed gave as the representative of the local Iraqi community. The media were seeking to add local content to an international story — bringing home the conflict to Canadians — and hoping to create a controversy. The reporters wanted to know what Iraqis felt about the invasion.

This was Majeed's chance. He could use a freedom of speech that would be unthinkable in his old country to publicize the dissenting views of the Iraqi community. After all, from the Iraqi perspective, Kuwait did not exist. Britain made it a country in 1961 — it was a British protectorate comprising a landmass carved essentially out of Iraq. The British had tried to control the Iraqis for decades as part of the Anglo-French plan to divide the Middle East after the First World War. The British even dropped chemical bombs on rebellious villages that did not pay colonial taxes and submit to the Crown. Kuwait was their ultimate punishment. Creating it left Iraq without a port on the Persian Gulf and kept British influence alive in a post-colonial sort of way. And besides, Kuwait had by then discovered that it had rich oil reserves.

"I said, 'Well, they [Edmonton's Iraqi community] are supporting the invasion, if you want to call it an invasion. The members of the community don't call it an invasion; they call it something different, that there was a coup in Kuwait and the Iraqi army was invited there.' " The media wanted to know if Majeed had any relatives in Kuwait. He replied that he had a brother who was an engineer in Kuwait and a sister and brother-in-law, both of whom were doctors. He told the reporters that he had talked to his relatives three times since the invasion and that the feeling he got from them was that most Kuwaitis were happy that the Iraqi army was there.

When the articles appeared, his phone started ringing off the wall. They were vicious calls from right-wingers and warmongers. He was stunned as they hurled obscene epithets at him, called him a traitor to Canada, and threatened dire consequences for his treason. Later in the morning, he started to get worried as some callers threatened to blow up his house and kill his family.

With most callers, Majeed could barely argue, and he ended up slamming down the receiver. One of them, although abusive, appeared to be the kind who was also willing to listen. He was a captain from the local fire department and insisted that Majeed's statement was an act of treason.

"I said: 'Sir, I want to meet you. You show me what you have done for this country, and I'll show you what I have done for this country.' I said, 'I would like to show you that I am a recipient of all kinds of awards, I am a member of the advisory board to the mayor and to city council, I am a member of the premier of Alberta's council, I am a member of the executive of a federally appointed [refugee] committee. And you tell me what you have received in your life.' " The captain demanded to know how Majeed could prove what he was saying, and Majeed politely invited him over. Majeed said when the man saw everything, he quickly apologized for his manner on the telephone. The two of them have since become good friends.

But most callers were not willing to listen to reason. Majeed decided to put on his telephone answering machine to monitor the calls and ended up with an hour and a half of hate.

"Then one day, I found something outside the house I had never seen before. I called the police, and they told me it was a pipe bomb — home-made," he said. At the time he lived in a condominium townhouse, which was built so that four houses were clustered in one unit. Had the bomb gone off, he said, it would have been a disaster, not just for him but for scores of others around him. Besides, his wife and daughter, who is disabled, were often at home. They would be the first casualties.

Majeed did not want to wait for another attempt. He decided to sell his house and move to another address. He would change his telephone number of eighteen years and pay to have it unlisted so that people couldn't just look it up in the phone book and also know where he lived. He was panic-stricken and wanted to move quickly. As a result, he lost $13,000 on the market value of the house.

The hate calls he had received and the pipe bomb left a bitter taste, but it slowly began to fade away as the weeks and months passed. Having moved to a new, unlisted address with a new telephone number, he felt secure. Like many others, he believed that eventually war would be averted. The massive troop buildup and the sanctions being enforced by the U.S. coalition would force Saddam Hussein to retreat. Again, he was wrong. The January 15 United Nations' deadline was fast approaching. And Majeed would soon find out that the worst was yet to come. Once the actual war started on January 16, Edmonton came down with a vengeance on its Arab and Muslim population. And Majeed's Tory friends began disappearing into the woodwork when he needed them most.

A racist backlash was unleashed at fathers and mothers, children and students, many of them from working-class backgrounds. According to Muslims at the Al-Rashid Mosque, not a day went by without talk about an incident in some school, Arab boys being harassed and pushed around or Muslim girls wearing the hejab being subjected to a torrent of abuse.

Majeed had already had one run-in with his son's school. Basil — a common Iraqi name pronounced Baasill — had written a poem that talked of peace in the Middle East and was sung to a rap rhythm. He wanted to read it for a local television station that was at the school to talk about the war. But the TV station was more interested in hearing messages supporting the Canadian troops in the Gulf. Basil then asked the school to publish his poem in its magazine. That too was turned down, and the principal informed Majeed that the school would publish it after the war was over.

Then, one evening, Kemal Majeed showed up home after school with his left eye swollen like a golf ball. He had been cornered by a group of white students and asked whether he was a Canadian or an Arab. "I am a Canadian, but my father is Iraqi and my mother is Lebanese," Kemal said he told the boys. "You better be," they replied. The next day after school, as he trudged home in the snow, about twenty students began pelting him with large snowballs as hard as rocks. One of them hit his eye. Majeed complained, and the school authorities promised to be more vigilant.

Two days later, Kemal was again cornered along with two other Arab boys by a student wielding what appeared to be a handgun. The student struck the other two boys and then told Kemal his turn was next, whereupon the frail boy, who looks more European than Arab, scrambled home to safety. This time Majeed was furious. He showed up at school only to find several other Arab parents there, complaining about harassment and beatings. The school refused to involve the police. Majeed decided he would call them himself since he knew both the police chief and the mayor personally, thanks to his involvement in their multicultural committees. The perpetrator was arrested.

Majeed knew that the backlash would worsen as the war went on. He would have desperately liked to see the bigwigs in the federal Conservative Party come to the mosque, go to Arab gatherings, and take not just a political stand but a high-profile public stand as they were shown mingling with the community. But the best he could get from them were platitudes, statements that berated racism and upheld the rights of Arabs and Muslims in Canada.

That wasn't enough. Majeed was begining to get a constant stream of complaints about increasing racist attacks as the war coverage on television became an evening spectacle. Majeed decided to limit his news intake to one news broadcast on television every morning. One Sunday, he finished his quota for the day and decided to take Kemal and Basil for a walk to the local shopping plaza in the Castle Downs area of Edmonton where there was a flea market. It was a weekly event where several vendors from the Arab and other ethnic communities displayed their wares in the bazaar fashion of the old country.

As the three were walking across the parking lot of the mall, they heard cries for help from an old Arab woman and her two young daughters. An aggressive white male had confronted them and was heaping abuse on them. He then tore the hejab off the mother's head, threw it on the ground, spat on it, and then began trampling it. Majeed ran toward the women as fast as he could. By the time he got there, the man had begun to heap abuse on Islam and Muslims. "What is your problem?" Majeed asked, only to have the torrent of abuse turned on him. The man then turned around, fled from the mall, and disappeared. Majeed was stunned. He had heard about several cases of hejab-ripping, but this was the first one he witnessed personally.

Hardly had Majeed recovered from this incident when he got a call one afternoon from an Iraqi man who was at a gas station near one of several mega food stores in Edmonton. The man's mother-in-law had driven to the superstore. As she got out of her car and approached the mall wearing her hejab, two men and two women, all of them white, jumped her. They ripped off her hejab, tore open the front of her blouse, and terrorized her for several minutes in broad daylight. While they were attacking her, consumers hurried by as if the incident was an everyday event.

Finally, the four whites left, leaving the woman shaking and in tears. "She sat on the sidewalk outside for about four hours, crying, shivering, I mean shaking, she did not know what to do, she was totally confused." At her home, the family realized that she had been gone for far too long. Edmonton was not Baghdad where a quick visit to the market usually ended up in visits to half a dozen relatives or friends. The son-in-law drove to the super-store and spotted the car. Not fluent in English, he called Majeed, who in turn telephoned the police. But the perpetrators had long since disappeared.

Majeed again looked toward his Tory mentors for help. But the government of Canada was demanding unquestioning loyalty to its war effort. And for those who wavered, it had some special measures, as Majeed found out when he tried to cope with the abuse his community was facing.

One day, as Majeed finished watching the morning TV news-cast and got his papers ready for what appeared to be a hectic session at the refugee board, the telephone rang. Majeed did not recognize the caller at the other end, which was unusual, since his number was unlisted. "Good morning, Mr. Majeed, I'm calling from the Canadian Security Intelligence Service," said the voice. CSIS has a mandate to search out potential terrorists, spies, and agents provocateurs. Since it has no powers to arrest, it works very closely with the RCMP and local police, in this case the Edmonton Police Department. And while the Arabs were making plans to protect themselves from racist attacks, selected members of the community were being targeted by CSIS and the RCMP for inter-views, based on input from the Edmonton police intelligence unit. Among those targeted was Majeed, the man who counted Edmon-ton's police chief as one of his friends. He was asked to report to a CSIS office.

He remembers that interview well. He found the manner of the CSIS agent questioning him haughty and rude. "How do you feel about Iraq's invasion of Kuwait," was the first question. "I said: 'Listen, before you ask me questions, I want to give you some background. During my studies in Iraq, we were always taught that Kuwait was a part of Iraq, until 1921. The British politicians decided that Iraq should not get access to the Gulf. They put

Kuwait there and brought in the Al-Sabah family [Emir Jabar
al-Sabah was the ruler of Kuwait who fled to Saudi Arabia with
his numerous wives during the Iraqi invasion], and they became
the rulers.' "

Majeed believes the CSIS questioning, which lasted more than
an hour, was harassment. Asked why he believes that, Majeed
replied: "Listen, I am a Canadian. When I was called, I had an
unlisted phone number, and they phoned me on this number. They
told me who they were. I said, 'I am busy.' They insisted they
wanted to see me. ... What were they trying to prove? I have done
nothing [wrong] in this country. I chose to come here, Canada did
not choose me. ... They asked me about certain activities of the
Arab community and ... about groups, parties; they knew everything, it was obvious, then why do [they] ask?

"They said, 'What do you think of Saddam Hussein?' What do
I think of this ruler or that person? What kind of a question is that?
We are Canadians. Ask me what I think of Pierre Trudeau, and
I'll say: 'He's a son of a bitch.' "

Majeed said they also wanted to know how the Muslims felt
about non-believers — Christian and Jewish troops — stationed
in the Holy Land of Saudi Arabia. Did it inflame him as a Muslim
to the point where his protest could become physical? When he
told them that this was a delicate question that must be decided
by religious leaders and imams, they said, "Oh, by the way, we
want to ask you about Imam Chebli." Majeed said they found it
strange that at one time Chebli would support Iran against Iraq
and, at another time, Iraq against the West. They could not fathom
Chebli's Islamic philosophy. "I said, 'Ask him this yourself.' I felt
this was provocation," said Majeed, pointing out that if the question were put to several Muslims it could well serve to drive a
wedge between the imam and his parishioners. He was right; it did.

Majeed said that he could well imagine the impact of a secret
service interview on the Lebanese who immigrated to Edmonton
between 1975 and 1991. Most of them were not well educated
because the continuing civil war in that country had shut down
schools. To survive, they had to join militias, to join militias they
had to carry guns, and if they carried guns, they had to kill or be
killed. Majeed explained that "they are always afraid of the
government. So when CSIS comes, it is like the Mukhabarat. If I
were one of those Lebanese without citizenship, I would say,

'What do you want me to tell you about Youssef Chebli?' And CSIS could put words into my mouth."

Edmonton's Arabs and Muslims were under siege. They looked around desperately for help, turning to people like Majeed to use their political connections, but no help was forthcoming. There were statements, such as the one from the mayor saying that she had instructed the police chief not to tolerate any acts of racism. And Joe Clark expressed his concern at the few incidents that the media had written up. But those remarks were wiped out by the prime minister in an address to the cadets at Kingston's military college. Brian Mulroney told them that it was crucial for all Canadians to unite behind the war effort. The implication, of course, was that if you didn't, you were not a loyal Canadian.

Not only could Majeed not explain away his party's policies, he also could not defend them without being completely ostracized from his ethnic constituency. And he decided he wouldn't. His political position was taking a 180 degree turn. "Canada is known as a peacekeeping country, but Mr. Mulroney proved otherwise, and Mr. Clark, what can I say about Mr. Clark? Every time he draws his gun, he shoots his foot, and after he shoots his foot, he puts his foot in his mouth." Canada had turned into a country where dissent was equated with treason and the ethnics who had posed for photographs with the elite when it was expedient for them to do so were easily expendable.

As Majeed sat down in his comfortably decorated townhouse one day and put all the pieces together, he realized quickly that the hopes he had built up around Brian Mulroney's Conservative Party had collapsed. He was not giving up on Canadians as a people; Majeed still believes that by and large Canadians are "beautiful people, generous and kind." He was only giving up on the Tory leadership, which had led Canada into its first war in almost four decades and sent its security forces after loyal citizens. He was giving up on a prime minister whose photograph would soon disappear from his living room. "Is this the kind of society we want to build? No, my friend. ... I am here because Canada is a peace-keeping country. We got into Canadian politics, we had our opinions added, it is all shattered, it was a dream, it is shattered."

The landscape of Canada is dotted with Majeeds, ethnic faces who adorn the political process like plastic decorations on a birthday cake, plucked out and put aside after the candles are blown out. Many of them offer their services willingly to bolster an image of Canada as a truly multicultural land, in return for positions on boards and committees and the sense that they are hobnobbing with the stars. When elections come around, beaming white politicians seek out their token ethnics and walk around their ridings. Majeed's case is the classic example of the often-repeated truism that political parties treat ethnics as tokens. While expecting total loyalty from their ethnic members, the commitment they offer in return is shallow at best. For years, Majeed was useful to the party. He brought in Arab votes for the Conservatives and gave the party an egalitarian image that quickly evaporated during the Gulf War. When the conflict began, Majeed became a liability.

His commitment to the party and his feelings for Canada made little impact on CSIS, whose agents questioned him like a common criminal. One has to wonder why he was targeted in the first place. He was a Canadian citizen, responsibly employed, and active in the community at large, at the municipal and provincial levels. If he was worthy of being targeted by CSIS, one must wonder if any Canadian citizen is safe from the prying eyes of Canada's Security Intelligence Service.

Could the Arabs and Muslims have done anything different? The question is largely rhetorical. They could have pooled their resources and mounted a country-wide campaign that might have forced Ottawa to tone down its pro-Washington war rhetoric — or, at the very least, forced it to rein in its security forces. But in many ways the Arab lobby in Canada reflects the Arab world. Differences are imported from the old country and played out in Canada, sometimes for selfish motives and sometimes to support the country of birth. There is no doubt that had Canada's Arabs and Muslims taken a united stand during the war, they could have significantly altered Canadian foreign policy.

CHAPTER THREE

Educating the Educators

"There are a lot of people who feel that this war is not over, it was just the first phase."

An Arab leader explains why many of those interviewed in London, Ontario sought anonymity

As the Gulf War began playing itself out, average Canadians gathered around their televisions to view the latest developments. Meanwhile, across the country, Arabs and Muslims listened every evening to the tales of harassment that their children were bringing home from school. It was almost as if the tormentors were eager to take the images from their television screens and turn them into firsthand experiences in the playground. Just as it became a ritual to watch the war hour every evening, it started to become a ritual in London, Ontario, every evening for Arabs and Muslims to listen to their children's stories and say soothing words: "Don't take it seriously; the other children don't know any better." In some cases, words were not enough, as Ikhlas and Cass, a working-class couple in London, found out when their son was provoked by his own teacher. What do you tell your offspring when their teachers behave like children? Arabs live by proverbs, and the one that sprang to Cass's mind during the anxious period went: "The eye cannot fight the needle."

During the Gulf War, many Arabs took solace in the fact that their civilization was more than a thousand years old. It would take time, but the Arabs in Canada would eventually be accepted.

Others, like Ikhlas, rejected such fatalism. Her philosophy was that she had given the best years of her life to Canada and deserved better treatment. Ikhlas is thirty-six, feisty and sharp tongued. She chainsmokes and dashes around in her car all day, but she makes sure the family home is run according to her rules. Her three children are fed Lebanese food and told about Arab culture.

Her family hails from the picturesque Zahle district in Lebanon. Sixteen-year-old Ikhlas was quite happy in her home town, Karaoun, when she suddenly found herself transplanted to Canada in 1971. Word had reached Karaoun that her aunt in London, Ontario, had been involved in a car accident. There was no one to look after her, and Ikhlas was asked to pack her bags and head six thousand miles away to a land that Asiatics and Middle Easterners still associate with the North Pole.

She helped her aunt recover, and then decided to stay on and work. In those days one could still apply for immigrant status from within the country. She worked in a factory and then in a bakery. On Sundays, she visited the mosque to meet other Muslims — the Arab and Muslim community then was too small for anyone to ask for time off on Friday afternoons, the mandatory day for community prayers in Islam. Life was hard but the money was good, and she saved enough to return to Lebanon in 1975 for a visit. While she was home, she met Cass, and they married. She told him about London, the quaint little city where people smiled at you and all the Arab families knew each other — much like Karaoun.

They returned to London, and Cass began driving a van for a linen-supply company. But London was growing, and the immigrant population in the city had increased substantially. Where once people were only curious when they met an Arab on the street, now they seemed threatened. After Ikhlas and Cass returned to London, the Canadian mosaic seemed about to crack. Paki bashings started in Toronto, with young punks seeking out any South Asian-looking person. And although Cass looked more Eastern European than Arab, Ikhlas was very much a visible minority, with her dark skin, black hair, and heavy accent.

Ikhlas said she could feel the friendliness of London being slowly eroded by a rudeness that manifested itself in how the mainstream dealt with the newcomers. She comments: "I find the mainstream community less tolerant. At the bank, I [am] not a

Canadian because I have an accent. Let me tell you about a recent incident. I and my cousin had gone to this mall. She had her kids with her. We sat down at this table and started talking. And this guy comes over. He says: 'You and you, if you are going to yap, yap, yap [in Arabic], you sit at the end of the mall. You can't sit beside us.' " Her cousin, who is as feisty as she is, got up and gave the man a piece of her mind, screaming that the mall did not belong to him, that they could sit where they wanted and speak in any language they wished.

Because of the change in Canadian attitudes towards immigrants, the two had earlier decided to give their children race-neutral names. The two daughters were called Reema and Nadeen, and the boy was called Shady. They chose these names because of the problems they had with their own. "Every time I would tell them my name, people would look sideways and say: 'What, what?' It made me feel so ashamed. I didn't want to put the children through that."

Cass had fewer problems because of his looks. His one complaint was also about his name; after sixteen years in the same job, his co-workers had still not bothered learning how to pronounce it. (Cass is not his real name. It is a nickname that is being used here at his request.)

When the bombing of Baghdad started, Cass encountered his first work-related problem. It involved a co-worker whom Cass had trained and who called Cass "my daddy" because of what the Arab had taught him. After the war started, he would repeatedly look at Cass and say, "Cass, we're gonna beat up on them Arabs." Finally, Cass grabbed his tie and yanked it. The man protested and said he had been joking. "Don't joke like that," Cass replied. "Or I'll put you in the [industrial] washing machine."

Ikhlas too had begun noticing a drastic change in the attitude of her non-Arab acquaintances. For one thing, they seemed to look at her as if she had a vested interest in something other than support for Canadian and other Western troops. The couple felt they had a lot to contribute to the war debate — they were from the region, they understood the Arabs, they read Arab magazines, and they could provide a balance that they believed was missing in the Canadian media. But they found it impossible to convince their non-Arab acquaintances. She explained: "People always said, 'We saw it on TV and so it must be true.' And that was that. You couldn't tell them anything."

They decided even before the bombing to keep their opinions about the conflict to themselves and only discuss it with their Arab friends and relatives. Unlike white Canadians, they were approaching the subject from a point of view that nobody seemed to want to hear. They were the progeny of Arabs who had suffered under a colonial past in a region that was suppressed and then deliberately fractured into countries that suited English and French designs. To them, Baghdad's invasion of Kuwait was the logical result of a colonial past that had artificially divided Arab nations and sown the seeds of inter-Arab rivalry. If history is also people living and breathing the past, how does one convey this experience to a blind population?

Being adults, Ikhlas and Cass could maintain this silent posture with non-Arabs. But there were the others in the family, their three children, for whom interacting with the chidren around them is part of growing up. And it was one of their children who drew the two out of their silence to confront the larger community. The Gulf War was brought home to them by their ten-year-old son, Shady. Shady is in Grade 5 in an elementary school attended by eight hundred students. The school is largely ethnic and has a large Arab population.

One day when Shady returned home from school, he was coughing and said he felt cold and feverish. Ikhlas asked him what had happened, and the story he told her made her blood rush to her head. In fact, the incident had started a few days earlier. Shady had come home and said a teacher had been going on and on about Saddam Hussein being a dictator, a Hitler, who had to be stopped with bombs; otherwise, he would take over the world. The teacher was clearly anti-Arab, and Shady felt uncomfortable. Ikhlas and Cass had told him at the time that he did not have to listen to the teacher because the Gulf War was not as black and white as some people were trying to make it out to be. So a few days later, when the teacher brought in a newspaper and again started berating the Iraqis and Saddam Hussein, the ten-year-old, who packs a tongue like his mother's, got up and challenged the teacher.

"He started to say all this stuff about Saddam Hussein is a dictator, a killer," Shady recalled. "And I said, 'How do you know he is a dictator; he is not trying to blow up the whole world.' And he started to yell at me. ... I told him, 'George Bush is a dictator, and if he is, then Brian Mulroney is a dictator.' And then I said, 'Is our principal a dictator?' and, I said, 'You are dictator. My parents told me I don't have to listen to this, I don't have to talk about this.' And my friend Kevin asked him why he was picking on me? Was it because I was Lebanese? And then he threw me out of the class."

The students were in a portable classroom. When Shady was asked to leave, he did not have his coat on. The temperature was about 15 degrees below zero. The boy was outside for about fifteen minutes and soon began to cough. When the teacher heard him coughing, he told him to report to the principal's office.

Shady has other recollections of the classroom. "He got some of the kids really scared because he said you have to take sides, because if you get a letter about the war ... you have to be in the war or you go to jail." The boy said on another occasion, when the teacher started to talk about the war and Shady told him he had attended a peace rally, the man started to yell at him again. Shady said he replied: "I bet George Bush is happy about this war ... because he is not in the war; he is just sitting down watching people die, and he is not doing anything. He doesn't really care who wins. ... He is sending out most of the blacks, not the whites; if he wants this war, he should go out and fight." Shady found that some of his friends were beginning to keep their distance from him because of his clashes with the teacher and his views on Saddam Hussein, which conflicted with the opinions they were hearing at home.

Ikhlas was furious, but she decided to be diplomatic. She went to the principal, explained what had happened, and indicated that she was furious, but she said, "Kids will be kids, and they are sometimes prone to exaggeration." She wanted the principal to get to the bottom of the story. Her approach worked. For one thing, it did not force the principal's back up against the wall. She got a wonderful response from the principal, who investigated, considered all the sides, and reprimanded the teacher.

Subsequently, the teacher apologized to Shady. The teacher's version was that he had asked Shady to report to the principal, but the boy misunderstood his instructions and stood outside the class instead and then exaggerated his account of what the teacher had said. After the incident, the principal went from class to class talking about the war. He showed up in Reema's class. Ikhlas had nothing but praise for what the principal said. He asked the children what they thought of the war. When one girl replied, "Saddam Hussein is a dictator," he asked: "Why do you say that? Have you read the other side's story? You shouldn't say this before hearing the other side. The Arabian people are very nice, and Muslims have dignity." Ikhlas said he spoke well of the community. She believes part of the reason may be his own exposure to this culture because his daughter was dating a Muslim boy.

The principal's conduct quickly made the rounds of the local Arab community because there had been other problems at the same school. But although Ikhlas and Cass were grateful for the principal's stance, the question remained: Why was a teacher with such views not punished more severely?

Jack Little, director of education for the London board, said there was some misinformation and exaggeration on the part of the boy and that once this was explained to the parents and the community, they were satisfied. "I am not excusing what happened," he said. "But you are never going to avoid all incidents." He concurred with the superintendent of the area that the teacher only needed to be talked to.

But many Arabs did not find this response adequate. Among those involved in Shady's incident was Massi, one of the executives of the Canadian Arab Society in London, who said the teacher should have been suspended to send a message out to others. He and others related the lesser response to the double standard that exists in government and media in dealing with the Arab-Israeli conflict. Their argument was, and it has some justification, that had the incident involved criticism of Israel and a Jewish boy instead of an Arab boy, the response would have been more substantial. What the Arabs were also forgetting, though, is the difference in the degree of organization in the two communities. With a long history of persecution, the Jewish community is much better organized to respond to any provocation that suggests bias. The Arabs clearly have a long, long way to go.

Unfortunately, Canadian institutions are not structured to hear the voices of silent minorities. And although the London board of education was very cognizant of the war and its potential for causing strife, its response was lukewarm. It was in keeping with the city's culture and history. London has been closely associated with militias right from its establishment. The city's first big economic stimulant was the decision of the British government to locate a garrison in the town after the Mackenzie rebellion in 1837. The city is proud of its military past and displays this segment of its history in museums and special parades that attract local schoolchildren.

Nevertheless, when Jack Little viewed the morning headlines on January 17, announcing the beginning of the war, he knew that the city's population had changed dramatically over the years and that they could expect some problems. He decided a meeting should be held with all the school principals to discuss contingencies. It would be a tricky business because Little had three constituencies to deal with. There was the Christian majority, followed by the Jewish community, which supported a war against Iraq, and then the Canadian Arab Society of London, which had been raising concerns about racism well before the bombing began.

The meeting with the principals ended up becoming very general, considering possible racist situations that could arise. Little said, "It was simply a matter of trying to make sure the values we have, which include respect for everybody, would be upheld at our schools." The meeting ended on a noncommittal note with board officials expressing the hope that principals and teachers would be sensitive to the needs of Arab students in dealing with confrontational situations, class projects, and discussions.

No specifics were laid out. For instance, simple questions remained undecided: Should teachers initiate projects that involved writing letters of support to the troops? What about the traditional yellow ribbons? Principals and teachers would have to play it by ear. Little said the board hoped they would take into account the sensitivities of students before setting up such projects. What about the tauntings and other incidents? He said it was impossible to avoid such problems because children simply repeated what they had heard in their surroundings at home. Perhaps he forgot that a major portion of a child's waking hours are spent in school.

The lack of a concrete policy in London ensured that any complaints moved slowly upwards in the heavily layered bureaucracy and died before being forced to a resolution during the war. The Canadian Arab Society demanded more concrete steps but felt that each attempt was spurned by the board. Just viewing the pre-war atmosphere in many of the local schools, Massi was certain that their worst fears were about to come true. His biggest conundrum was: How could London's twelve thousand Arabs fight a leftover colonial mentality in this city of three hundred thousand, with streets that bore names like Black Friars and Oxford, with its tea houses and its scones and its white establishment?

Massi met school board authorities to organize a seminar that could help sensitize teachers to the Arabs and their special needs. He said a superintendent assigned to deal with him rejected the idea, saying the board did not want to be associated with any such thing. She pointed out that even having a moment of silence in schools for all the victims of the war — which was ordered by the provincial education ministry — had drawn irate phone calls from Londoners.

They called the move an "unpatriotic gesture" since the coalition was there to "kick ass" anyway. The Arabs were told they could have the seminar once the war ended. They argued that the decision smacked of racism since native Indians were allowed to host such a seminar after the uprising in Oka, Quebec, in the summer of 1990 and the Jewish community was also given the opportunity after a case involving a Western Canadian schoolteacher who had been preaching racism against Jews. Little denied that there was any bias in refusing to organize a seminar. He said it was more a matter of logistics, bringing together thirty-five hundred people in one place. He said the Arabs were told that they could organize a seminar and that the board would leave it up to the teachers and principals whether they wished to attend or not — making it a voluntary affair.

Eventually, the board allowed the Arabs to distribute some written material to teachers. Much of it was put together by the Toronto-based Near Eastern Cultural and Educational Foundation, a group comprising university professors and intellectuals, and it was culled from articles published in the mainstream and alternative press. However, Little took exception to some of the material, claiming it was too one-sided on behalf of the Arabs — he had other groups to contend with.

The Arabs continued lobbying and eventually obtained a public statement from the mayor, Tom Gosnell, that racist incidents would not be tolerated in the city. About two weeks into the war, the board of education finally agreed with the mayor's suggestion for a meeting of Arabs, Jews, and Christians to discuss racism in the schools. It was held in the Atrium — a large hall, which is a public area in the middle of the school board building. Little does not know how it happened, but when everyone got there, they found the meeting had become a press conference.

Unprepared, the Arabs cringed as reporters shoved micro-phones in front of them. They should have used this opportunity to gain publicity for the community and for the school situation, but they had come to distrust the media because of their coverage of the war. Even Little admits that a lot of what some principals, such as Shady's, were doing was being neutralized by a one-sided coverage of the war. But the board did nothing to correct this inequality, treading a careful path in order not to upset the far more powerful Christian and Jewish lobbies. The board's actions were reactive — putting out the fire and hoping that they could do so before the flames spread. In short, the board gave up.

And the fire began spreading as other schools began experienc-ing their share of problems. At Shady's school, a Palestinian boy was teased by his fellow students. "Here comes an Iraqi, here comes an Iraqi" was the chant in the playground; then, some older boys came over and beat him up. At another nearby school, Ikhlas had to intervene in the case of a seven-year-old Arab boy who came home for three days in a row with a black eye. The boy's name was Hussein, a very common name among Muslims. Ap-parently, Hussein's schoolmates watched television at home every night and then beat little Hussein black and blue every day. It was Ikhlas who persuaded the parents to go to the school and take action to stop the beatings.

But one of the sadder cases was recounted by David Hassan, who heads the local mosque committee. The teacher of a young Palestinian girl asked the class to write letters of support to the Canadian forces in the Gulf as part of a class project. The girl's family was in Kuwait, which was being bombed by the U.S. coalition at the time. She objected, but she was told she would have to write a letter or lose marks. One evening she sat down and wrote the letter of support. Along with the letter, she wrote a note to her father, which she placed by his bedside that night, saying words to the effect: "Please forgive me, but my teacher forced me to write this letter, and if any of our family is killed, I will never forgive myself."

The anguish suffered by Shady and the other Arab children in London was unnecessary as well as appalling. And if one were to plot a graph of blame, it would finally arrive at the school board, which had neglected its policy-making responsibilities and had left decisions to the individual opinions and preferences of its principals and teachers. It was like giving each staff member a drum. They could beat it how and when they wished, creating a medley of disharmonious sounds that ranged from a march to a mournful roll. The only guiding principle was upholding the value of "respect for everybody." But what does this phrase mean? If thirty of thirty-five students believe that opposing the Gulf War is tantamount to treason and therefore deserves a beating in the sandbox, can the board turn a blind eye? Can the teacher then force the five to write letters of support to the troops as a class project?

London's School Board might have based their response to the Gulf War on Canada's Multiculturalism Act of 1988 and stated at the outset that given the multiracial makeup of the country, it would endeavour to remain neutral in the dispute, regardless of the measures that Brian Mulroney had initiated in support of Washington. It could have then banned teachers and principals from organizing any war-related projects — immediately excluding yellow ribbons and letters of support for troops. Such a ban had already been imposed by Metro Toronto school boards where any supportive actions were left to individual students and not encouraged by schools. Teachers could have been warned not to impose their views on the students, regardless of whether they were doves or hawks. There could have been guidelines for war discussions in class — to make sure the stand taken by both sides was made clear. Parents should have been warned that racial taunting would be met with disciplinary action — a special appeal should have been made to Arab and Muslim parents to report incidents immediately.

Yet Jack Little has said he would not handle the situation any differently were it to arise again. It might then have been worthwhile for the policy to be dictated by the province. When Ontario mandated that all schools observe two minutes of silence for the war dead, Arab and non-Arab, the board fielded hate calls from right-wingers, passed the buck, and blamed the province. Still, the two minutes did teach the students one important lesson: the ultimate horror of war.

CHAPTER FOUR

A Heritage of Discontent

"I thought Kuwait was a fruit that came from Australia, until the Gulf conflict started."

A Hamilton nurse, talking to an Arab patient

M unicipal councils don't usually discuss wars, restricting themselves instead to community concerns such as development and property tax. And yet the Gulf War was on the agenda of Hamilton council. But then Hamilton, Ontario, is known for three things: its steel factories, its air pollution, and its racism, a phenomenon the city has been battling since 1985. The council debate focused on the spate of racist incidents that surfaced as the bombing of Baghdad got underway. Sane voices on council were calling for peace and racial harmony when alderman Tom Murray, a weight-lifter, volunteered his solution, "Nuke the buggers." His remark was reported by the media.

Although Hamilton has its share of citizens like Murray, fortunately it also has individuals like Bernadette Twal, a third-generation Canadian who sits on the city's race relations committee. Bernadette is bent on discovering the heritage and culture of her Lebanese ancestors. She is also bent on defending the rights of Arab and Muslim Canadians. During the Gulf War, she was slowly pushed to centre-stage, her notepad filled with a list of racist incidents that began in her own household. It was a sad discovery for her that four generations do not a Canadian make.

Bernadette Twal, petite, blonde, and pale skinned, is the forty-
one-year-old daughter of Fuad Shebib (an anglicized version of
the Arabic Shabeeb). Fuad, or Edward as the folks in North Sydney, Nova Scotia called him, was a second-generation Canadian.
His father, Farjallah, a shoemaker, came to North Sydney in about
1904 to join his brother George.

When Farjallah died, Fuad was thirteen and in Grade 8. The
family decided he should work at odd jobs. When he was older,
he learned music and joined a company in Chatham, New Brunswick, as a peddler, selling guitar lessons. It was on one of these
selling trips that he met his wife, an Irishwoman named Kathleen
Ryan. It is a story that Bernadette loves to relate. Fuad arrived at
her mother's home to sell guitar lessons; Kathleen opened the
door and replied, "No, we have a piano." As she tried to shut the
door, he put his foot in the doorjamb saying, "Lady, don't fool
me; no piano can fit through that door." He came back the next
day with an actual guitar — presumably to serenade Kathleen.
The two were married and moved to Halifax, where Bernadette
and her four brothers were born.

Bernadette has mixed memories about growing up in Halifax
with a name like Shebib. It stood out along with the food she ate
at home — Kathleen had quickly mastered an all-Lebanese
cuisine. Bernadette's friends would turn up their noses at Lebanese delicacies such as kibbi, a patty made of finely ground
meat mixed with herbs and spices, marinated and eaten raw — a
Lebanese steak tartare. Or yogurt — in those days yogurt was not
in style. She remembers fooling one of her friends once, telling
her it was vanilla ice cream and putting a spoonful in the girl's
mouth.

She grew up hearing tales about Lebanon, about her ancestors
who were farmers in the old country, growing lentils and other
produce. She heard about the wondrous hills and valleys, about
Zahle, about the people, the coastline. Fuad had lost all his Arabic,
and the one thing he could not teach his children was the language.
But he constantly reminded them of their cultural legacy and told
them never to forget it.

When he was getting close to sixty years, Fuad's passion for
his ancestry overcame him. He had moved to Hamilton in 1970,
and he began frequenting local Arab gatherings. The word spread
that there was a man with a big nose who could not speak a word

of Arabic but claimed to be an Arab. His eagerness and pride in Arab culture soon made him a very special person in the community. For the first time, he met Muslim Arabs. As an Orthodox Christian, he had grown up mistrusting Muslims. Even Bernadette remembers her history lessons at St. Thomas Aquinas School and at St. Patrick's High School, both Catholic schools in Halifax, learning about the Crusades and the Holy Land and getting a picture of Arabs and Muslims as a shifty, backward bunch.

Fuad began learning a little Arabic. And suddenly, it was as if he had found himself; a second-generation Canadian had become a Canadian Arab. As if to regain a lost lifetime and a lost heritage, his one plea to Bernadette was, "Marry an Arab." Bernadette had no qualms about that. All the stories she had grown up with had instilled a thirst in her for the Arab world that led her to dream of Lebanon in colour. In 1974, she met Ramzi Twal at a lecture by Elmer Berger, an anti-Zionist rabbi, at the local university, and in 1976 they were married.

It was through Ramzi's experiences that she realized for the first time that to rediscover her ancestry she would first have to cleanse it in the minds of other Canadians. Ramzi, a Palestinian who came to Canada from Jordan in 1966, was a product of extreme racism, and he remains pessimistic. For him, the experiences of Arab Canadians during the Gulf War were simply a continuation of the existing state of things in local and national institutions. The cases that he and Bernadette heard while they served on the municipal race relations committee came as no surprise.

In 1985, Hamilton had erupted with serious race problems over discrimination faced by South Asian cab drivers. The local taxi company either refused to hire them or acceded to demands from customers that they be sent cabs with white drivers. The issue was settled after a lengthy human rights hearing. Out of this was born a municipal race relations committee headed by the mayor and Harish Jain, a professor of business studies at McMaster University. Jain is a world-renowned scholar of race relations and employment equity. The idea of the committee was that it would provide an avenue to handle complaints and resolve them informally before they got caught up in the bureaucracy of the provincial human rights commission. Jain, who was initially asked to head the committee by himself, refused and asked the mayor to co-chair it. His thinking was that without the mayor the group would not be taken seriously by city council and the local government.

The committee had thirty-eight members, but there were no Arabs on it, even though there are more than ten thousand Arabs and Muslims in Hamilton. When Ramzi and Bernadette applied for Arab representation, they faced opposition from the Jewish community. Jain remembers creating a fuss about that. "When the Palestinian husband and wife applied, yes there was some concern. People stereotype Palestinians as terrorists," he said. "I and the mayor felt why should we have this committee if you are going to keep people out because some people feel that they are terrorists. I could say the same thing about those people, and so let's not get into the back-home politics; we are in Canada."

Then, some of the members raised the issue of the credentials of whoever was going to represent the Arab community. Ramzi was furious. "So," he said, "provide me with the resumé of everybody on that committee," and they said, "No, that is not your prerogative." And he said, "It is not your prerogative either [to question us]. If we want to put a donkey on the committee to represent us, his or her qualifications are up to us as the Arab community. ... We are always coming in to defend ourselves; we are always seen as aggressive."

Bernadette began serving on the race relations committee along with her brother, Peter Shebib, who represented the powerful Steelworkers' Union. She continued on the committee during the Gulf War. It was at one of the race committee meetings that Bernadette realized the serious situation created by the war. One day a white woman came up to her at the meeting and started describing what she had faced. The woman had gone to a local supermarket, and because it was a cold day, she had wrapped her head with a scarf. Apparently, the scarf was not unlike the Muslim hejab, and the woman at one of the cash registers refused to serve her. "You people are the cause of all our problems," the cashier screamed at her and walked away. The woman had come to tell Bernadette that if such an incident could happen to her, a white woman, "then I can imagine what it's like for your community."

Bernadette became a kind of central repository, working during the day at a nursery school and collecting cases of Arab harassment in the evening. As the representative for the Arab community, Bernadette detailed these cases at the race committee meetings.

She had more cases than she could talk about. There was an eight-year-old Arab boy who refused to go to school after hearing a teacher talk about Saddam Hussein killing little babies in Kuwaiti incubators. (Amnesty International had originally put out the story as an allegation made by Kuwaitis, but subsequently retracted it after finding out that it was unsubstantiated. Meanwhile, the media never stopped mentioning it.) Her own niece, Lisa Shebib, didn't go to school for two or three days after the war started because she was sick of constantly hearing Arabs referred to as barbarians and terrorists.

In a high school, a white boy was allowed to abuse Arabs while the teacher just looked on. When an Arab boy got up and told him to shut up, the teacher ejected the Arab boy from the class without trying to find out what his concerns were.

At another high school, two Arab boys were suspended for a week for fighting a group of whites. The two had intervened when a gang of whites jumped an Arab boy in the hallway and began beating him up. At the time this book was written, the boys were still appealing to the school board to have their suspensions removed, and Bernadette was fighting their case. The parents did not speak English well enough to argue it themselves confidently — a condition that would afflict many Arab families during the war.

Children were not the only ones who were harassed. Bernadette also heard many cases involving families. In one instance, an Iraqi family heard a crash outside their front door. When they looked out, they found that a black garbage bag with rotted food and beer bottles had been flung at their home. Another Iraqi family told Bernadette about calls they were getting at 3 A.M. in which a man would say, "Get out of Kuwait or die," and then hang up.

And then there was the case of Maha Amery, a young Lebanese Muslim married to a doctoral student, Hussein Amery, at McMaster University. Maha is a twenty-year-old teaching assistant at a local school. Maha was shocked to hear some of the most hateful statements directed at her race coming from the teacher for whom she worked as an assistant. One teacher said that Saddam Hussein was crazy and that she hated Arabs. "I said, 'Why,' and she said, 'Look what they did to the Israeli people, and look what he did to the Kurds.' And I said, 'Did Israel care when she hit Lebanon [in its 1982 invasion, killing thirty thousand Lebanese and Palestinians]?' " Another teacher expressed glee when U.S. jets bombed the civilian bunker near Baghdad, killing Iraqi women and children.

Maha was furious. One day, the teacher, realizing that she might have hurt Maha, asked, "Maha, do you like Jewish people?" Maha said she wanted to hurt the teacher as badly as she had been hurt, and so she replied: "No. You don't like Arabs and I don't like you; I don't like the Jewish people." From that time the teacher realized Maha had been hurt and did not talk about the war.

At the same time, her twenty-one-year-old brother-in-law, Ali Amery, was being asked by his fellow students at Mohawk College: "Where do you keep your machine gun? How many people did you kill today? Are you gonna go over and fight for Saddam Hussein?" Ali often thought that they weren't joking, but he glossed over the remarks. The one incident that remains etched on his memory came during the lunch break one day. He was sitting and chatting with a woman he had known for two years. Suddenly, she jumped up and said: "You're an Arab! How can I trust you?" Ali said he was stunned into silence and had no reply.

But Bernadette did not have to go far to find out what the other Arabs and Muslims were facing. There was the case of her own son Najeeb, a ten-year-old. It started off with his bus driver telling the children a war joke: "What happens when you spell Saddam's name backwards? It comes out: Mad Ass." The children squealed with laughter, except for Najeeb, who went up to the driver and complained that she was using swearwords before children from kindergarten.

When he got to school, the name-calling began, with children saying he was a Palestinian geek, a terrorist, and Saddam Hussein. A girl came over to him and asked if he was going to bomb them. He responded to the girl by saying: "What's it to you? Maybe I will bomb you." But on the third day, Najeeb's resistance started to wear down as the students launched into a new tirade and began calling him "A-Rab, A-Rab." Bernadette said he came home and "he cried and cried. I've never seen him cry so hard. It was like his heart was broken. Until then I thought he was taking it really well. He did not want to return to school, and we had to talk to his principal."

Najeeb then began developing sleeping and eating disorders — several Arab parents reported these problems among their children. He hardly ate, and where he used to fall asleep at 9 P.M., he now lay awake until midnight. There were bags under his eyes. Then there was his fear that the authorities would arrest his parents for being Arab. On television and radio he heard about security precautions to prevent Arab terrorism in Canada. Saddam Hussein had asked Muslims and Arabs to revolt, and the immediate assumption in the media was that the community would automatically respond.

Then one day there was a telephone call. Najeeb is at the age where he likes answering telephones. Even the outgoing message on the answering machine is recorded by him in his shrill young voice. He picked up the phone, and a voice at the other end asked for Ramzi Twal. His father took the call, and Najeeb ran, half screaming, to his mother: "It's the police, it's the police. I know they're gonna take away Dad." He could hardly control his emotions. Bernadette tried to pacify him. It was, in fact, the police, calling about a theft at Ramzi's carpet store. They were seeking details about one of his employees.

For Najeeb, battling prejudice at such an early age was a loss of innocence. According to a Montreal psychiatrist who has handled cases resulting from war trauma among children, Najeeb was displaying the typical symptoms of a child who had internalized the conflict. The views of those he loved contrasted with those at school from whom he sought acceptance. He became irritable and withdrawn, easily provoked into a fight, and he showed a reduced self-confidence and sense of security.

What was happening to the Arabs in Hamilton and elsewhere was nothing short of a "nightmare," to use the words of Harish Jain. As co-chair of the anti-racism committee, he desperately wanted to do something concrete as Bernadette was repeatedly requesting. But what could a local government do except make such token gestures as asking Mayor Bob Morrow to come out with a public statement about equality and justice, asking Arabs and Muslims to complain to the authorities more often, and asking the police to go after wrongdoers.

But the Hamilton-Wentworth Regional Police, whose members sit on the race committee, was itself co-operating with the RCMP and the Canadian Security Intelligence Service in determining national security threats from Arab Canadians. The Hamilton force is white dominated, and the number of minority police officers does not represent the visible minority population — they make up 4.5 per cent of the population of the Hamilton-Wentworth region. Until recently, the force, backed by Alderman Tom Murray, did not allow Sikhs to wear turbans as part of their uniform, though doing so is a religious requirement in the Sikh faith. The race committee could expect little sensitivity from the force.

Jain said he was told about cases where the security forces would go to Arab homes and show them photographs of peace marches they had joined, asking them why they had done so and demanding that they identify other Arabs in the demonstration. Jain comments: "We advised people to co-operate with the police, with CSIS, if they have reasonable questions, because as Canadians we want to protect this society ... but co-operating does not mean ... Arabs being visited and shown pictures and asked if they participated in this and this demonstration. This is a free country, for God's sake, and just because you and I participate in demonstrations doesn't mean I am against Canada."

Jain heard cases of white Canadians telling first-, second- and third-generation Canadian Arabs to "go back where they came from." He notes: "Many of these people escaped oppression to come here. This is the only country they know. What do you mean, 'Go back where you came from?' " To battle racism during the Gulf War, he would have to begin in Ottawa, with Canada's foolhardiness in joining the war, with a national media that appeared to be ripping and pasting articles generated by a biased media in the United States. He soon realized that there was little his committee could do.

His remarks betrayed a certain helplessness about finding an immediate solution when all the elements of a local government cannot act with the kind of commitment shown by the race committee. Jain and the mayor could ask the people of Hamilton not to be suspicious of Arabs. But the next day, the national media would quote federal Solicitor General Pierre Cadieux asking Canadians to be vigilant about subversion, since Canada was in a state of war. His remarks would smear the very people whom Jain and the mayor were trying to shield.

The only other institution to which the race committee could turn was the media. A local reporter from the *Spectator* did call Bernadette, she said, after her presentation to city council. But he sought more precision about the episodes she was describing so that they could fit into the high-tech format of the war coverage, with computer graphics and coloured charts. "He said, basically, 'Nobody is going to believe you unless you give me names and dates and times.' And I said: 'I can't give you names, there is a confidence involved, there is a fear there, they feel they won't be dealt with fairly, they may have to suffer more later on. ... Do you think I am going to city hall to tell fairy tales?' "

The reporter, obviously under pressure from his editors, said he understood but that there was nothing he could do. "I told him, 'That's just too bad, but I can't give you any names.' And so the paper wrote in general terms that I made a presentation that there was a backlash in the community. There was no byline on the story either."

The race relations committee decided to hold monthly multiracial gatherings as one way of promoting harmony in the community. The first such meeting was held after the war, on March 21. Children representing different ethnic groups were at city hall, talking about their experiences in Canada. With the war over and the pressure off, the meeting also got a very good response from the media in the form of generous coverage. Among those speaking was Najeeb Twal, narrating his experiences and making a statement for which he would become famous in the community, "I'd rather be called Saddam Hussein than George Bush. I take it as a compliment."

Professor Saleem Qureshi of the University of Alberta in Edmonton has a favourite saying that typifies the dilemma faced both by the Arabs and Muslims and by the municipal race relations committee: "Leaders make policies and the people pay the price." What could the committee accomplish? Its success in previous instances was directly related to the local issue at hand. The taxi company whose practices were discriminatory fell within its ambit — the local government controlled taxi licences — as did the case of a black woman who had been denied a nursing home licence. But what could it do about a war against a foreign population, scores of whose members resided in the area?

At best, it could appeal to Ottawa to take a more neutral stance in future situations. It could berate racists and ask Hamiltonians to be more tolerant. It could ask the school board to be wary of incidents and respond to them more sensitively. It could ask the police to chase the perpetrators more aggressively. And then it would have to sit back and hope that the locals were paying more attention to it than to the national leaders appearing on television asking Canadians to unite behind the war effort. It was a crapshoot with loaded dice.

CHAPTER FIVE

To Serve and Protect

"I ask Canada and the people of Canada, 'Why do you open your doors to another population to come here, and then you make war on their country, and you show hatred to those people here.'"

Canadian Iraqi Mikha Yakow questions
multiculturalism in Canada

One of Fares Yakow's earliest memories of Toronto is the motto of the Metro Toronto Police, which is emblazoned on the side of the force's white police cruisers: To Serve and Protect. Fares is a seventeen-year-old Iraqi Canadian who lives with his two younger brothers and his parents in the Rexdale district of Metro Toronto — an area where large, featureless apartment buildings dominate the surrounding suburban homes, and strip malls, take-out restaurants, and convenience stores compete for the remaining space. It is a rough area, given its poverty. The large ethnic population is resented by the white working class, which doesn't take kindly to multiculturalism.

Fares immigrated to Canada in 1983 from a country where authority is feared. His family had heard about justice and even-handedness in Canada, where the law takes its own course, and the outcome is not dictated by a person's ethnic origin or status in life. He grew up watching popular police dramas on television and peering at the face of the smiling police officer at his school talking about Elmer the Elephant's rules of road safety. Like the other children in his class, he soon came to admire and respect the

police, believing that where there was a uniform, there was little
to fear.

The Gulf conflict was a rude awakening for Fares and his
family. It taught them, among other things, that sometimes the
force is confused about whom it is serving and whom it is protecting. His family learned the hard way that there is a law for the
rich and a law for the poor. When the chips are down, an ethnic
family of modest means can expect to be put near the bottom rung
of the justice ladder.

The Yakow family immigrated to Canada from the village of
Al-Qush in northern Iraq, a Chaldean Christian farming area that
is dominated by Kurds. The Chaldeans are among the earliest
Christians. The Yakows describe with pride how the Chaldeans
were the first to accept Christ. It is a tightly knit community, even
in Canada, but not a rich one. In Iraq, Chaldeans and Assyrians,
another old Christian sect, are among the foremost supporters of
Iraqi President Saddam Hussein, and they are as patriotic as the
Muslim majority.

Financially, life was not unbearable for the Yakows in Iraq.
Mikha Yakow, the father, drove a truck, and he would sometimes
earn as much as $300 in a day. Mantaha spent the day visiting the
bazaar, dropping in to see her sisters, aunts, and friends but getting
home in time for Fares and Jinan when they returned from school.
Fares himself has fond memories of his home town, the simplicity
of life, the friendliness of the people — a place where he could
dash into any home if he needed help and was guaranteed a
sympathetic reception.

But like thousands of other Iraqi families, the Yakows were
uprooted from their homeland by the Iran-Iraq war that started in
1981. Several of their relations were in the Iraqi army. They were
at the front to sustain an invasion begun by Saddam Hussein with
the blessings of the West. It was intended to break the back of the
first real Islamic country to be established in centuries.

The Yakows — Mikha, Mantaha, and their boys, Fares, who
was nine, Jinan, eight, and Basil, four — fled Iraq and arrived in
Italy, where they set up their home in a refugee camp. From
everything they had heard, Canada was their choice for settlement
— after all, any country that had not fought an offensive war in
four decades and only sent its forces out as peacekeepers must be

built on a lot of human kindness. They lived in makeshift housing in Italy for sixteen months, while they went through the Canadian selection process. Finally, the family headed for Toronto, the home of several thousand Chaldeans.

In Toronto, both husband and wife had to work hard to make ends meet. Mikha worked in a furniture factory while Mantaha, who had learned woodworking, became a cabinet-maker, specializing in kitchen cabinets. She enjoyed her work so much that she would sometimes put in a twelve-hour day, and she often worked weekends. In her spare time, she made cabinets for their apartment and proudly displayed them right next to the dining-room table. The two slowly began decorating the modest three-bedroom apartment where they continue to live.

Mantaha's job ended abruptly one day when she was told by the manager that she would have to start making a heavier type of cabinet. In addition, she would also have to lift the cabinets by herself and stack them one of the top of the other. The woman protested in broken English that this was "a man's job" and that she couldn't do it. Her $11-an-hour job was immediately terminated. Later, she found out that the factory owner had hired a group of Latin American refugees at $6 an hour and was looking for an excuse to fire her and several others.

By that time, the couple had saved enough to purchase a Becker's convenience store franchise. Mantaha began looking after the store, which was near their apartment building, and often Fares and Jinan would go over and help. But Becker's charges much higher prices for the goods it sells than other stores, and this did not sit well with customers in the largely working-class area. Many would fling the goods back at Mantaha after learning the price and curse her for charging "cut-throat" prices. Often people came in drunk and swore at her because she could not speak English well. One day, she said, she saw one of the customers pocket a magazine. She quickly locked the door and called the police.

Meanwhile, the man had begun to curse her and threaten her for locking the door. When the Metro Toronto police showed up, she tried to explain what had happened. Emotionally high-strung as a result of being locked alone in the store with a belligerent, abusive man, she became even less coherent. She expected some support from the white policeman, but he obviously had little patience and dismissed her charges as false.

When she described how the thief had sworn at her, the officer replied: "This is a free country. People can use the language they want." She said she began shouting at the police officer, unable to control herself after months of facing abusive customers. She told the officer that if he did not do something, she would sue, she would complain — although she had no idea how she could do this in Canada. He replied that she could take his badge number and complain; he couldn't care less.

The couple decided to sell the store in 1990. The same year, Mikha was hurt at the factory, suffering back injuries that forced him to quit. He had hardly applied for worker's compensation when Saddam Hussein's army marched into Kuwait, and the mood of Torontonians began changing towards the Iraqi community.

At first the media and then the Canadian population got caught up in the euphoria of the high-tech war machines that Washington was amassing in Saudi Arabia and around Iraq. And when Ottawa sent its ships to join the Americans, the war finally came home to Canadians. As the media ran story after story about the Iraqi brutality in its occupation of Kuwait — much of which later proved to be propaganda — public support for the war began to build. Iraqis were now the enemy, and not merely abroad, but at home as well. This image of Arab Canadians as the enemy would be tolerated in many schools, and Father Henry Carr Catholic School, which Fares and Jinan attended, was one of them.

Both brothers began to face racial taunts at school from the other children. In class, they would seethe with anger as other students poked fun at Arabs in general. It was especially unsettling because Fares, who was now seventeen, and Jinan, who had turned sixteen, had settled down well in school. Their speech bore no trace of an accent, and they mixed freely with the other students. They had begun learning about the history and culture of their new country.

Jinan, who was in Grade 11, also had an aptitude for electronics, and he often helped a white friend of his in class. The two had become good friends, but their friendship began to sour as the war loomed closer. In early November, the student who used to seek Jinan's help began cursing him as an Iraqi. "You and your brother are Iraqi shit," the boy told Jinan. Jinan lost his temper and warned the student to watch his tongue. Later, the boy took Jinan's seat in class and refused to give it up, using obscenities to describe Jinan's family. A scuffle ensued before the teacher asked the friend to report to the principal.

That evening, as Jinan and Fares were walking home, the boy came up with a group of friends and shouted at them, "Go home, you Iraqi shit." Jinan said he then tried to punch him, and they got into a fist fight. The school suspended them both for two days. When Fares broke up the fight, the boy told him, "Tomorrow it's your turn."

On November 27, 1990, when the two-day suspension period had ended and Fares and Jinan were walking home, they were accosted by the white boy's cousin outside the school. He said, "You messed around with my cousin." Fares said the boy tried to push Jinan, but he intervened and said it was all over.

"No, it's not," said the boy, and suddenly Fares and Jinan were jumped by a gang of ten or twelve white youths. In keeping with the Arab tradition of protecting his younger brother, Fares screamed at Jinan to run to the principal's office for help. Jinan escaped, and looking over his shoulder he saw Fares being knocked to the ground by the gang and covering his face with his hands. At one point, one of the boys punched Fares so hard he fell backwards onto the road, almost falling under a car that was passing by. Fares was incredulous. The driver stopped and was joined by people from several other cars.

"They just stood there. I couldn't believe it. None of them even bothered to help stop the fight. There were ten of them beating me up. I felt so stupid; they just stopped and watched. This guy hit me, and I almost fell in front of this car, and he stopped and watched. In Iraq, they would have stopped the fight, even if they knew they could get killed. This is why I don't like Canada; nobody cares about anybody else. And the police did not take me to hospital, did not call an ambulance ... and why take information if you're not going to use it? Who are they serving, and who are they protecting? Before this, if I were to see a person fall, I would help him. After this, I won't help anybody. I feel like that now. If I were to see a person die, I wouldn't help him."

Jinan said people were watching the fight from the window of the principal's office. He waved at them and screamed that they should call the police, but he was ignored. He then went into the office and described what was happening, and the police were called. Two cruisers screeched to a halt where Fares was bent over. The boy could hardly stand up, he was bleeding, and his face was bruised. The police demanded a statement from him, took it down in a bureaucratic fashion, and left the scene. He would have to visit his family doctor for treatment, they said; he did not look too bad to them, just shaken up.

Because of the beating, Fares was late returning home. Worried, Mantaha decided to go over to the school. Pregnant at the time, she walked slowly until she saw Fares. His face was bloated to almost twice its size, his eyes and his nose were black, and his chin was bleeding profusely. The boy stood outside his school on the street with no energy left. A teacher had given him some ice to shrink the swelling. "What happened to Fares," Mantaha demanded. The teacher told her nonchalantly that some ten teenagers had given him "a hard time."

Mantaha rushed the boy to their doctor, who fixed his bruised chin with stitches and quickly enrolled him for physiotherapy after prescribing some painkillers. Fares was devastated, mentally and physically. He wanted his parents to pack up and leave for Iraq as soon as possible; he had had it with Canada. He did not think the country was a suitable place to bring up his two younger brothers. Half crying, he described to his parents how he had been beaten up by a gang with no help from the school authorities or passersby or even the police.

Fares said he told the two policemen everything. "I gave them our Iraqi background, I told them about the taunts, the racism, about being called Iraqi shit, about the fight with my brother. I gave them the name of the boy involved. Later, I called them up, and gave them the full names of some of the boys, and even some addresses. I kept calling them up, and they kept saying they were investigating and investigating and investigating."

Four months after the incident the police had not laid a single charge. They eventually told the family on the telephone that there was nothing they could do and that they were dropping the whole matter. Two weeks after they dropped the case, some members of the same gang showed up again at the school and taunted the two boys. Fares said he again called police, who essentially said it was the boys' problem; he and his brother would have to protect each other.

Fares had a premonition that racism at his school and elsewhere would escalate once an actual war started. He was right. Almost every day, Jinan and his twelve-year-old brother Basil would consult with Fares about how to handle situations in class and in the playground.

The three boys were now being harassed regularly at school, and the parents did not have a sufficient command of English to challenge the teachers and the principal. Even Basil was gloomy. He had been nicknamed Scud by his classmates after the infamous Iraqi missiles.

Jinan is very apolitical and decided to keep mum in class, not venturing an opinion even when the students heaped abuse on Iraq and Iraqis. But Fares decided to take the offensive on the war. He began standing up and challenging his teachers in class. He started putting forward the Iraqi point of view about the theft of oil and the fact that Kuwait was an Iraqi province until the colonial powers took it away and made it a separate country. But it was a losing battle, he said, because the others would simply point to newspaper articles and television commentary to justify what they were saying. "The one thing I could not take is when students would say in front of the teachers, 'Why don't the [Canadian] Iraqis go back where they come from?' And the teacher would let them say it. One of the teachers talked of Israel as the big hero, the most powerful nation in the Middle East. Even the theology teacher made fun of Iraqis and said Iraqis should be flushed down the toilet."

At one stage, Fares approached his parents and said he wanted to drop out of school; he couldn't take it when both the students and teachers were abusive. Mikha and Mantaha convinced him to stay on. And so he decided to take another route to make his point. He prepared a class project on Iraq. In the context of a learning institution, his project should have been considered invaluable: it offered a wealth of knowledge about another region of the world from a live source, discussed the history of the region, the people, the economy, growing up in Iraq, his village, the historic Tigris River, the colonial takeover of the region, the creation of Kuwait, and Iraq's justification for invading that country.

"It's my country and I must tell the truth," said Fares, who visited Iraq in the summer of 1990. "When it comes to Israel and Palestine, then Canada is the peacemaker. But when it comes to Kuwait, it joins a war." He said his teacher found the project good, but a strange thing happened. He was never given any marks for it, whereas everybody else was assigned grades.

The beating that Fares suffered at the hands of the other students came at a time when the Metro Police had announced special enforcement to deal with escalating youth gang violence in Toronto. And yet Fares's beating was ignored. The Yakows are convinced that the lack of response resulted from an inherent racism on the force. In addition, the Yakows, being Iraqi, were viewed as the enemy within Canada. Does an enemy have any rights, especially in a war situation? The Yakows lived in a poor area, spoke little English, and could hardly muster the political clout needed to motivate institutions in Canada. Had the same thing happened to a white boy from an upper-middle-class family, it is more than likely that someone would have been charged.

Even if the force could not pursue the beating, for whatever reason, the two officers could have asked Toronto's ethnic relations unit to visit the family and explain the force's reasoning. The unit has Arabic-speaking officers whose pictures are proudly displayed on a poster that the force publishes to show its sensitivity to minorities. But that would mean taking on an extra workload for the officer involved, given the number of refugees and immigrants moving into the area where the Yakows lived. It would mean more work and few brownie points from his platoon commander.

In addition, according to insiders on the force, paranoia prevailed, with many members of the force convinced that there was a terrorist threat from Arabs and Muslims. Members of the police intelligence unit were freely discussing domestic terrorism with the media, which were running their assessments under large headlines, all of them aimed at Arabs. One candid officer, who did not wish to be named, said: "You can't imagine how biased [many white officers] are toward Muslims. They even suspect Muslim officers on the force. And then you have the RCMP, which thinks there is a terrorist conspiracy at every mosque and in every Arab home." The Mounties were using the ethnic intelligence files of the Metro Toronto police extensively to pursue their investigations, as they were in most other cities.

According to officers close to the Toronto police force's intelligence unit, there were no serious or real threats of terrorism, only paranoia among the Mounties and senior white officers. The closest the force came to any incident was a telephone call made to a synagogue by a Pakistani Muslim with a history of mental illness. He threatened to bomb the building in retaliation for the mass killings of Muslims in Iraq. A man at the synagogue kept the Pakistani talking while the call was traced. According to police sources, the man convinced the Pakistani that his threats were misguided, and the caller had begun profusely apologizing for making the threat when he was arrested.

The incident reveals the double standard that operated during the war. As soon as the Gulf War started, police began visiting synagogues and Jewish institutions to offer advice on security. Conversely, James Kafieh, president of CAF, had to call police himself before some officers showed up to give his organization some points on securing their building from threats of retaliation. Some officers also visited mosques and other buildings to talk about security after garbage and excrement were flung at them. The officers took advantage of the opportunity to seek out information on local Muslims. In the minds of the security forces and the local police, Arabs and Muslims constituted a threat to Canada, while the anger vented at these minorities was dismissed as the unfortunate but logical outcome of Canada's participation in the war. The presumption that the country's Arabs and Muslims should be treated as loyal and innocent until proven otherwise had vanished.

During the Gulf conflict, Arabs and Muslims perceived an indifference on the part of local police forces to their complaints. The community was let down by the media and by many of the school boards, they could not turn to their local governments, and, of course, Ottawa's priorities excluded these minorities To lack the support of the police as well in apparently clear-cut cases of assault was alarming. Unfortunately, the Chaldean community was not organized enough to form a delegation and seek special protection from the police. The incident with Fares made the rounds of the community, creating even more fear among its members, who decided to circle the wagons and protect each other. The first public airing of Fares's plight was at a meeting between External Affairs Minister Joe Clark and Canadian Arabs in late January, midway through the war, when a local Chaldean leader accused the government of causing the racist backlash by joining the war and engaging in war rhetoric. By the time of the meeting, the incident was old news, and the media were not interested.

The lack of sophistication in this community, and among many other minorities in Canada, becomes even clearer when one considers that the Yakows did not realize that they could have pursued the matter after the officers had dropped it and not have been cowed into submission by the police. Neither Fares nor his parents had any idea that the force had an internal complaints process or even an ethnic relations unit. When I told him about these possibilities, Fares decided that the matter should not end with the decision of a constable. He got in touch with the Canadian Arab Federation. CAF President James Kafieh got in touch with the police's ethnic relations unit and made it clear that if a satisfactory explanation wasn't forthcoming, CAF would seek a probe of the matter. The police would have to account for their behaviour toward this seventeen-year-old Iraqi Canadian, regardless of Canada's stand in the Gulf War.

Imam Youssef Chebli photographed after a Friday sermon in Edmonton's Al-Rashid mosque. Behind him is the *mimbar,* or altar, on which Muslim imams, or religious leaders, deliver the Friday sermon. His family was subjected to harassment and death threats because he applauded Saddam Hussein for standing up to America and supporting the Palestinian quest for a homeland.

The Al-Rashid Mosque in Edmonton.

The Chebli family poses for author Zuhair Kashmeri. From left: Mohammed Chebli, his mother Maria, and father Imam Youssef.

Ferial Elatrash was interviewed by two RCMP officers after someone reported a distorted version of a conversation. She complained to the RCMP's public complaints commissioner. At the time of publication, her case was still being reviewed.

Fares Yakow, seventeen, stands outside the Father Henry Carr High School in northwest Metro Toronto, on the spot where he was beaten by ten white teenagers. Passersby and motorists stopped to watch.

Bernadette Twal comes from the well-known Shebib family, which includes famous Montreal film-maker Don Shebib. This family picture was taken in Sydney, N.S., just after her grandparents' immigration from Lebanon in 1904. Top row, from the left: her three uncles, Michele (Michael), Yousef (Joseph), Jameel (Jimmy). Centre row: grandmother Annie with uncle Albert on her knee; and grandfather Farjallah with Eva on his knee. Bottom row: her father Fuad (Freddie) and aunt Rose.

Abdullah Massih Thomas was the commissioning engineer for Ontario Hydro's Pickering Nuclear Station. During the Gulf war, CSIS interviewed him. There had been talk of terrorists targeting nuclear stations.

Left to right: Mohammad Amin, a Montreal psychiatrist and head of the Muslim Community of Quebec, and Amer al-Roubaie, an economist, stand outside the MCQ mosque and Islamic elementary school in Montreal. Amin helped Muslim adults and children cope with trauma and harassment caused by the war. Roubaie, a long-time Canadian, was questioned by CSIS, because he is a volunteer at the mosque.

James Kafieh, head of the Canadian Arab Federation, poses outside a Canadian Armed Forces fighter jet. He is a former fighter pilot with the Canadian Armed Forces. During the War, he fought the RCMP and the Canadian Security Intelligence Service over their harassment of Arabs.

James Kafieh holds up a front page of the Toronto *Sun* at a conference on "The Gulf War and the Media," organized by Toronto's alternative radio station CIUT. The headline, "Iraq Agents Here," refers to a story that claimed that the FBI believed there were twelve Iraqi saboteurs in the Toronto area. The FBI denied having such information.

Baghdad Travel, in the north end of Metro Toronto, is the official agent
for Iraqi Airways. During the war the twenty-foot sign outside was
smashed and fell to the ground. The owner, Mouschel Odishou, was
interviewed by CSIS, Canada's spy service. Because of the police focus
on the store, its clientele dried up and he had to declare bankruptcy.

WHEN CSIS CALLS

An Arab Canadian Guide
To Civil Rights

Produced by
Canadian Arab Federation

When CSIS Calls is a brochure published by the Canadian Arab Federation. It was widely distributed to Arab groups during the Gulf War.

CHAPTER SIX

Maintaining the Right

"You can look at any spot in Metro Toronto to be a target. There are many places where a terrorist could attack to make their point known."

Toronto police Inspector Jim Neish of the intelligence unit in an interview with the *Sun*

If the Gulf War was taking its toll on Arabs and Muslims, it was also taking its toll on Canada's institutions. Among them was the RCMP. With all the rhetoric about domestic terrorism that was circulating in the country, the RCMP brass made it clear that the force was implementing a national plan to counter any threat. It was called the National Emergency Operations Plan, and it would be implemented in the case of a national insurrection. It involved setting up a national command post — in this case the RCMP headquarters in Ottawa — and breaking up the country into several regions. Each region had its own command headquarters and several hundred investigators and intelligence officers. The intelligence and information collected by these men and women were forwarded to Ottawa, which generated a daily summary for the government. Headquarters also analysed the information from the regions and from other sources such as CSIS, Customs and Immigration, the U.S. Federal Bureau of Investigation, and the government itself.

The RCMP's efforts to avert the possibility of terrorism would take officers to strange places at strange hours and, in many cases, unannounced. The element of surprise was essential, they maintained, in case there was a terrorist to be caught.

Many of the RCMP's forays into the Arab community left even individual Mounties wondering what they were doing. One officer said in a candid conversation that it also left them embarrassed. "If you can only imagine the look on the faces of the people when we knocked on a door and then flashed our badges. Most of these were unsophisticated people who were trying to figure out their next month's rent, and here we walk in … without a warrant." Some Mounties would joke with their interview subjects to excuse themselves for being in their homes in the first place. Others would take their visit seriously and make sure they left behind a chilling effect. Some would end up in arguments. But, the officers knew that sooner or later they would come across a sophisticated Arab Canadian who would raise a fuss. They were right. When the complaint finally came, it was made by a charming young woman who works as a secretary and case-aid worker for the Catholic Children's Aid Society in Etobicoke, a Metro Toronto suburb.

Ferial Elatrash looks younger than her twenty-four years. The only features that betray her Arab background are her large black eyes and her name. Otherwise, she could easily pass for Spanish or Portuguese. There is nothing Arabic in her apartment either, with its modern furniture and large floral prints on the walls. Ferial is a product of the Toronto school system — she grew up in that city after immigrating to Canada with her parents when she was barely four years old.

Her earliest memory of Toronto is the lights. The memory is as distinct today as it was twenty years ago when she was flying into Toronto from Tel Aviv with her Palestinian parents and her sister. She remembers leaning over in the plane and seeing the lights everywhere; she had never seen so many lights. Like thousands of other Palestinian children, she was transported from her place of birth to another city, in Ferial's case from Beit Sahour to Toronto, a city that was fast becoming a United Nations.

Her parents settled in the west end of Toronto, in the Christie and Bloor neighbourhood, which continues to be very ethnically mixed. Soon, she was enrolled in school, and she picked up English quickly. Ferial remembers that her parents wanted the children to learn English and grow up fully Canadian with no trace of their Arab background. She forgot most of her Arabic, and any early memories of Beit Sahour were erased from her mind.

Like other immigrant families, the Elatrash family constantly tried to better itself by moving to improved accommodations. Each time, Ferial found herself in a different school. She remembers one school where the student population was largely West Indian. When the family moved to the Weston area, she was in a school with a white majority, but she had no problems. The family was Orthodox, but they attended a Protestant church, and, besides, Ferial did not look Arab.

Only in high school would she suddenly realize the extent of racism in Canadian society, and this experience shaped her responses to her surroundings after that. Her high school had a mix of West Indians, Italians, and other whites. Often, she said, two factions would join up to take on the third. Or, sometimes, everybody would join together and get ready for "the big rumble" with the kids from the Catholic school next door.

By the time she turned twenty, she was convinced that racism was inherent in Canadian society. She experienced it personally when, for seven years, she dated a West Indian black. She says she will never forget the comments they would hear on the buses, from both communities. The whites, mistaking her for one of their own, would openly tell her in public that she "could do better." Some blacks would tell her boyfriend to find somebody from his own community.

As a result of her experiences, she slowly turned into a fighter, battling racism, and she began to drift into politics. After high school, she joined the NDP and began working in its campaigns and attending its meetings, where her awareness of racism further matured. She joined the riding executive of Ontario Premier Bob Rae and worked in the election of 1990 that saw the NDP win a majority for the first time in the history of a province that had consistently elected either the Conservatives or the Liberals.

But there was one thing that Ferial never did. She never told anyone that she was a Palestinian. She would say that she was born in Israel or that she was of Arab descent. "I thought people would think of me very differently and automatically group me in with the PLO [the Palestine Liberation Organization] or what was going on in that part of the world. I only saw one side of it, I never saw what was going on in the West Bank, how the Arabs were being treated, because my parents did not instil that in me. I only got what the media was putting out, which is that the Palestinians are terrorists. ... I considered myself Canadian, which is right, but at the same time I should have kept my heritage, which I never did."

Although her parents did not discuss her background, her uncle and aunt did. By her early twenties she started feeling comfortable with the idea of being Arab. She still did not know the language, but she loved Arab food — although she did not know the names of most of the dishes. She is very close to her aunt and felt the anguish along with her when the woman's teenaged nephew was shot and killed by an Israeli settler in the occupied territories. But, except in the presence of her aunt, she would always say "Israel" when she was asked where she was born.

After high school, Ferial attended a community college before joining the Catholic Children's Aid Society as a secretary and case-aid worker. It was close to what she wanted to do in life, and there were real people to help. She continued to volunteer her services to the NDP, and in keeping with their stand on the Gulf conflict, she threw in her lot behind the peace movement.

"I don't believe in war ... I believe that Canada should not be involved. I did not want Canadian troops over there, because it was not our war ... and I don't want the government spending all this money [almost $1 billion] to send the troops over to kill ... when this money can be spent in our own country. ... I did not agree with Saddam Hussein, but there had to be another solution than war."

In her office, as in hundreds of others in Toronto, there was a split in thinking. Many sided with Ottawa and Washington and questioned Ferial's stand. However, she had a minority on her side who defended the position of the peace movement. One of her defenders, a woman, joined Ferial in a demonstration organized by the Toronto Disarmament Network and other peace groups outside the U.S. consulate on January 15.

That demonstration drew hundreds of protesters who marched from the consulate to the Progressive Conservative Party's local headquarters nearby. There were students from schools and universities, office executives in suits and ties, leftovers from the hippie generation, and other ordinary Canadians who disagreed with the massive troop concentration around Iraq. The demonstration was well covered by most of the media except the *Globe and*

Mail, which ran only three paragraphs the next morning. There were TV crews and still photographers, not all of them legitimate news media people. A Metro Toronto Police officer said many of them were filming for either the Metro Police or the RCMP. The demonstration was dominated by white Canadians. Ferial and her girlfriend were among the hundreds who signed a petition that was sent to Ottawa and no doubt ended up in the hands of the RCMP once the war started the next day.

Many of her friends and co-workers thought she was crazy to attend the demonstration. Ferial said she was shocked to discover how many people, including many of her friends, supported the war and believed that the Iraqis had to be neutralized. Many would argue with her that she could not claim to be a loyal Canadian and at the same time oppose the war. But Ferial continued supporting the peace movement.

Then on January 26, there was a knock on her apartment door. It was a Saturday, and Ferial had invited two friends to come over for supper. Since it was nearing 8 P.M. and they were due any minute, she was rushing to finish the pasta sauce. She was puzzled that her friends had not buzzed her from the main entrance, but she thought that a neighbour had let them in. She quickly straightened her clothes and rushed to the door to greet her friends. When she opened the door, she found herself staring at two men, one dressed in a suit and tie and the other wearing a sweater. Both had their badges ready to flash at her, and they quickly announced that they were from the RCMP.

"My heart dropped. When they first said RCMP, I thought something serious had happened to a family member. They said, 'Can we come inside?' And I said, 'Has something happened?' And they said, 'No.' They wanted to talk to me. Then it clicked in because I had been watching TV and talking to my relatives about the RCMP and CSIS knocking on Arab doors. I said, 'I know exactly why you're here, and I have nothing to say to you, and you have no reason to be here. I am offended.' I wanted to shut the door, but they flashed their badges at me and said, 'Do you know who we are ... we are the police.' "

She said she still refused to let them in until they said they had "a public complaint against me stating that my family or myself may be a threat to Canada during the crisis in the Middle East." They refused to elaborate on the complaint. It struck Ferial at the time that she was right next to the elevator and it was a Saturday night when people constantly come and go. "I was becoming embarrassed, and I did not want my neighbours to think that they had an Arab terrorist living in their building."

Eventually, Ferial let the officers in. They made themselves at home on the sofa before she could shut the door, and when she turned around, she found their eyes wandering all over the living room. But she was regaining her courage, mixed with a lot of anger and other emotions.

"I just didn't give them a chance to talk, I didn't, I was so angry, I was shaking. The week before when I was discussing this with my family, I said there was no way I would let them in; I would tell them where to go and send them on their way. That's what I said, and here I was letting these two men in, and there was absolutely no reason for them to be there. And they made me feel intimidated, and they were sitting in my living room and making themselves at home. I said to them, 'This is racism,' and one of them started to chuckle and laugh. They continued to tell me about this complaint, saying, 'This is a public complaint, and we have to investigate all complaints.' "

They refused to specify the complaint or name the complainant, except to repeat that it involved terrorism. Ferial said she asked them whether they had checked into the complaint before knocking on her door. She said they replied that they had and that everything "came up negative." She shot back at them, "Then why are you here?" Ferial said the two laughed, and to lighten the atmosphere, one of them said words to the effect, "To see if you have any hand grenades hanging on your window or posters of Saddam Hussein on your walls."

Ferial said she started laughing with them, but she remained angry. She noticed that the two were looking embarrassed, and she again asked them to elaborate on the complaint and tell her who the complainant was. She said the officer in the suit and tie replied: "Well you're probably ... not going to sleep for a couple of days wondering who would do this to you. Do you have any enemies?" At the time, Ferial believed that they picked her for one of two possible reasons: either someone she knew had complained about her anti-war stand, and since she is of Arab descent, that made her a potent combination in the imaginative eyes of the

Mounties; or, they had gone down the list of names on the peace petition, picking out Arab names.

However, as they spoke to her, they apparently decided that she was not their idea of a terrorist plotting to blow up a Canadian installation. Suddenly she stopped laughing and asked the two, "Is this what you do on a Saturday night? Go knocking on Arab doors?" They replied, "No, we knock on other doors too." It had been about ten to fifteen minutes since they had shown up, and she asked them to leave, which they did. They gave her their business card. It bore the name Const. G.T. (Gary) Mandville, Investigator, Immigration and Passport. Below that the officer in a sweater and no tie had written, Constable Gibson. Just before leaving, one of them sniffed the air and said, "Gee, your dinner smells good." Ferial had completely forgotten about supper and found that she had burned the pasta sauce.

Soon after they left, her friends arrived to find her angry and shaken. They discussed the incident, but its impact did not sink in until later. "The worst part of it was the feeling I got after that; I felt like I was being watched, everywhere I went, I really did. I had the feeling that somebody was following me, everywhere. What kind of check did they do on me before? Were they following me? Did they bug my phone? I was afraid to use my phone. That's how they make you feel. I started looking underneath my couch, where they sat, trying to see if they had left something. It all starts to play tricks on you. I didn't sleep that whole weekend. I am on the main floor and I felt somebody could be looking through the window."

Toronto had two rapists on the loose at the time of the RCMP visit, and the Metro Toronto Police had issued an alert. That added to her anxiety as she thought over the interview and chastised herself for not checking the peephole first to see who was outside before opening the door. What she was going through is described by criminologists as the "chill factor," a feeling of fear and paranoia that results from such a visit by the forces of the state.

Ferial wanted to fight back as she had done in every other instance. She sat down and jotted notes about what had happened in those fifteen minutes and called her MPP, the premier of Ontario. She left a message on his answering machine, and Bob Rae called back. He expressed concern, but he did not say much, she said, except to offer to help her draft a letter of complaint to the RCMP.

Meanwhile, she related what had happened to her friends, and the response from many of them shocked her. They believed the RCMP were justified in checking out the complaint. She remembers visiting a friend's relatives for dinner. The relatives listened to her tale and then told her that they could not chide the RCMP for doing what they did. They knocked on Arab doors for the protection and safety of all Canadians. Ferial said to top it off, these people were Italian, a community that had faced the threat of internment in Canada, when Mussolini joined the Second World War.

When Ferial told her parents, they were upset but philosophical about it while her two brothers, who were born here, and her sister, whom she describes as more Canadian than she is, treated the visit as a big joke. Her uncle and aunt took it more seriously. They laughed, but only because they could not figure out why she was targeted. If anybody, they should have been picked out because they were active in the Canadian Arab Federation.

The incident changed Ferial's life in many ways. For one thing, she began spending more time with her aunt and asked her to go through Palestinian history with her, so she could soak up a culture that had been denied her. She knew a lot of Arabic words, she thought, and decided it would not take her long to learn the language. That would be another project.

The incident heightened her interest in politics, and she decided she would go back to school and enrol in several courses. The incident did not make her feel any less Canadian. In fact, she was even more fired up to take on the challenge of securing equality for the minorities in Canada and become an advocate for the people.

But another realization suddenly dawned on her, one that her parents had hoped she would never have to face. She realized that she was not a white Canadian and would never be accepted as one. The pretending had to stop: it was time to hyphenate herself and make Canada live up to its charter of rights. And so, the next time people asked her where she was born, she did not say Israel or simply Beit Sahour. "I am beginning to learn," she said, "that the proper reply is Occupied Palestine."

On January 30, four days after her interview with the two officers, Ferial dashed off an emotional letter of complaint to the RCMP's public complaints' commissioner. She wrote that she found the visit offensive, "an unjustified action by the RCMP. I feel very angry that my rights as a Canadian citizen have been violated. The fact that I was not born in Canada does not make me any less of a Canadian. This is indeed a racist action by the Canadian government. Have we not learned from our mistakes of the treatment of the Japanese in World War II?" Ferial demanded an investigation, that the results of the investigation be communicated to her, and that she receive an apology from the RCMP.

Soon after she sent the letter, she met James Kafieh. He gave her his card and suggested they get together quickly since CAF had begun accumulating other evidence about harassment by the RCMP and CSIS. CAF obtained a lawyer for her, J. Robert Kellermann, a civil rights activist from the Vietnam era when American draft dodgers were escaping to Canada. A short hearing was held to obtain more information from Ferial, and the commission then returned to Ottawa to decide whether it would investigate.

On February 14, her case was raised in the House of Commons' external affairs committee by Svend Robinson, a New Democrat member of Parliament from Vancouver who has spent his career fighting for civil rights and for minorities. He was incensed, repeating the allegations from CAF that the Mounties and CSIS were going on a "fishing expedition." Later, he recalled that one of the things that disheartened him was that he could not sustain the momentum. He needed more ammunition to keep hammering away, but CAF was not organized enough to give him the information he needed.

He continued to raise the issue, but more on moral grounds and in a general manner that could be quickly brushed aside by smooth-talking Tory-appointed bureaucrats and ministers. He said in the committee hearing about the targeting of Arabs: "A number of these individuals, who are Canadian citizens, have come from countries in which a knock on the door without any phone call ahead of time can engender a great deal of fear and apprehension. Even what some might consider a routine visit from police authorities can be seen as a form of very serious harassment."

Robinson did elicit a favourable response about the Ferial case from RCMP Commissioner Norman Inkster, who told the committee that if her version of the incident was accurate, she had good reason to be outraged. But Solicitor General Pierre Cadieux had a ready-made reply to dampen Robinson's concern about Ferial: It was under investigation and so he could not comment.

The minister could have stated that the government would get to the bottom of the whole matter to reassure Canadian Arabs and Muslims. He could have reiterated and re-emphasized the statement by Inkster, and he could have publicly ordered the security forces to act more sensitively and responsibly. But obviously the government had a different agenda. It needed desperately to galvanize Canadians behind the war effort — polls had shown that a majority of Canadians did not favour an offensive role for Canada. Subtly pointing a finger at Arabs and Muslims was one way of informing Canadians that whether they liked it or not, they were surrounded by enemies who could do them grievous harm. In reality, neither the government nor the police believed this to be true. Individual police officers laughed at the memos that came down from headquarters. Ferial's incident was yet another case that showed that the national emergency plan had been employed to create an emergency rather than to tackle one.

The complaints commission did eventually agree to investigate Ferial's case. But the wheels of justice grind slowly, especially when the system itself is on the receiving end. Four and a half months after her complaint, on June 6, Ferial's lawyer, Robert Kellermann, got a letter from the complaints commission asking one question, "Did Ms. Elatrash at any time and either in a serious or joking manner make a comment directly or indirectly to her art class teacher that she and/or her parents and/or other family members were intending to travel to the United States for the purpose of blowing up or damaging in any way a nuclear plant in that country — more particularly in the State of Nevada?" (A June 11 letter asked the same question but added the words: "to her art class teacher or others in the class.")

Ferial was stunned. She contacted the teacher, who confirmed that all Ferial had told her in an anxious conversation was that her mother and her uncle were flying to Nevada for a holiday during the war and that she was worried about the trip. She was anxious, she had told the teacher, because of the threat of terrorism in the United States and because her mother would be so close to this massive nuclear plant. The teacher told Ferial that she had not complained to the RCMP because there was nothing to complain about. If the teacher hadn't reported Ferial, then it had to be one of the handful of students who had overheard the conversation and let his or her imagination run wild in response to Ottawa's plea that Canadians should be vigilant.

Kellermann said: "The real matter is: Do you show up at the home of a citizen and bother her, without investigating what a person may have overheard and reported? It's ridiculous if the RCMP jumped on every rumour and every statement. The manner in which they operated raises the issues of racism and of freedom of speech. I think they had no basis to do what they did to her." Ironically, her mother and uncle did travel to Nevada to get away from the bitter cold in Toronto. And U.S. Customs and Immigration did not question them, even though her uncle has a Jordanian passport.

Ferial Elatrash faced the double disadvantage of being both a woman and an ethnic. During the war, she faced yet another hurdle — being targeted by the RCMP on hearsay as a potential terrorist. For most of her life, Ferial has been a Canadian citizen; she works at a responsible job and is very involved in Canadian life and politics. The sudden appearance of two Mounties at her door, their pressure to be admitted into her apartment, and their questions qualify as a clear violation of her civil rights. In addition, one can only wonder at the attitude of many Canadians who supported intrusions of this kind and believed that since Canada was at war, the security forces were justified in targeting Arabs and Muslims at random.

However, if anything mitigated the harassment of Arabs and Muslims by the security forces, it was conscientious politicians like Svend Robinson. As a politician, Robinson never flows with the stream, and he has a record of never backing down from the principles of civil and human rights he has always fought for, right from his university days in British Columbia. Within a week of Robinson raising Ferial's case, the public complaints commission decided to accept it for investigation, although it took its own time. At the time this book was written, it was still going back and forth between the officers and Ferial. But meanwhile, of course, the war had ended, the Iraqis were humiliated, the Canadian troops had returned to a tumultuous welcome, the yellow ribbons had come off, and Ottawa was gloating over its role in fighting a war for freedom and democracy.

CHAPTER SEVEN

The Business of Terrorism

"One threat that may not be readily apparent comes from Iraqi, Arab or Palestinian sympathizers living in Canada who may not agree with Canada's role in the war."

From an article in the *Financial Post* of Toronto, warning its corporate readers to think security

One of the most graphic metamorphoses that Canadians went through during the war was the questioning of Arab and Muslim loyalties. People who had been loyal employees were suddenly looked upon with suspicion. "Better safe than sorry" became the order of the day. A private company that serves Toronto airport laid off two Arabs, purportedly as a cost-cutting measure. An Arab draftsman who worked for an oil company in a city west of Toronto had been promised a transfer to Montreal. Suddenly he was told that the move was cancelled and that, in fact, he was being laid off along with two others.

The public sector was no better. A senior bureaucrat in Ottawa, who is from Egypt, found that his reports were being questioned. "I have ten years of impeccable recommendations, and none of my decisions were questioned," the man said in an interview. "During the war, every report was violently questioned. I could absolutely feel the difference. These were people who may have posed two questions in the past but were now going for the jugular."

He was not the only Arab with an impeccable service record whose loyalty was questioned during the Gulf War. Just outside

Toronto, a Chaldean Christian from Iraq faced a similar fate. Abdullah Massih Thomas, a senior engineer at the nuclear power station in Pickering, also found himself under a microscope. Unlike the other three, Thomas came out bellowing with rage at everybody from External Affairs Minister Joe Clark to the security authorities.

Thomas is a sixty-year-old, six-feet plus, robust individual, whose deep voice drowns out all others around him. He lives with his wife Victoria in Ajax, a small town about forty-five minutes northeast of Toronto, in a country home on ten acres of open countryside. Four of his six children still live with him, and the family, although settled in Canada for twenty-five years, still maintains most of its Iraqi traditions in language and in food.

For Thomas, who is from the town of Al-Qush in northern Iraq, life has been a blessing. He studied in the United States — although his parents made sure he and Victoria made contact in the traditional Chaldean way and were married before he left for his studies, lest he return home with an American wife.

Thomas began thinking of immigrating to Canada in the mid-1960s when he was working as an engineer in Kuwait, but when his immigration to Canada was approved, he turned it down. Then, he decided he would leave for Canada after all to give the children a better education, and he wrote to the nearest Canadian immigration office, which was in Vienna. He was told that he would have to come for another interview. He replied that if that was the case, he would forget about it. Eventually, the immigration office decided that they would make an exception for Thomas, given his speciality in turbines. His immigration was approved automatically from the old file.

In Toronto, he decided to reject an offer from Westinghouse, his employer in Kuwait. It meant he would have to be on the road for weeks, leaving his young family behind.

Instead he went to a personnel agency. The man there was impressed by his qualifications and immediately called up a company that had registered with his firm. As Thomas sat across from him, the man told the client company: "I have just the guy for you; he's a very highly qualified professional engineer who has worked eight years in thermal power plants. He knows all about pipes and fittings. His name is Abdullah Massih Thomas." Thomas said there was a pause as the man at the other end said something, and the placement officer replied, "But he doesn't look like an Arab." Thomas said he grabbed the telephone and told the voice at the other end that he would not take his job even if it was the last one in the country.

Instead, he accepted a position with Ontario Hydro, a provincial government corporation. His first posting was in Deep River, a small town in Northern Ontario, in the middle of winter. There was no Orthodox Church in Deep River, so Thomas drove to the Roman Catholic church on Sunday, the family dressed up in its best. After mass, he waited for Father Buckley, the local priest. He went up and presented himself, and introduced his wife and six children — he had had another one since coming to Canada. He said the priest looked at the well-dressed family and asked Thomas whether the large car parked in the driveway was his. "Did you say you were immigrants?" Thomas said he replied: "Father, I am a professional engineer. Why do you assume that every immigrant must show up with a begging bowl?"

In 1969, Ontario Hydro offered Thomas the position of commissioning engineer for a very special project — he would help build the Pickering Nuclear Generating Station near Ajax. Thomas accepted immediately and took up the task, helping build the power plant from its very inception.

After Pickering was built, Ontario Hydro asked him to stay on, and he became a senior engineer involved in running the plant — a stamp of appreciation for his loyalty and hard work. He liked the Pickering area, the children were growing up, and he did not want to move. Besides, the Chaldean community in Metro Toronto was increasing substantially, and they wanted him to become the head of their association. He enjoyed being around a community that he could call his own, meet at a rented Catholic church on Sundays, discuss old politics, and simply shoot the breeze.

Despite his senior position at the Pickering nuclear station, Thomas did not change his views about the Gulf conflict one iota. He maintained right from the outset the legitimacy of Iraq's claim to Kuwait and totally disagreed with the stand taken by Canada. For Thomas, it was history correcting itself. Kuwait as a nation had never existed; it had always been a part of Iraq and needed to be joined to its motherland.

He would argue with his co-workers, friends, and others about the righteousness of Iraq's position. There was no way he could share Ottawa's indignation at the invasion of Kuwait. "Where was Ottawa when the Palestinians were being slaughtered by Israelis on the West Bank and Gaza? What Ottawa was doing, he said, was joining the West to make war against both Christian and Muslim Arabs. "I am not a Muslim, but when I see all those Muslim children being killed by Israel it hurts me because I am a real Christian and I worship God and I know the Muslims worship the same God ... the Christian and Muslim religion is the same ... read the Koran, Sura [chapter] Maryam [Mary] and it is the same ... Jesus came from the will of God and so on ... the only difference is that we say he died and three days later he rose and was sent to heaven and the Koran says when the time came to be crucified ... God would not let him be crucified and so he lifted him up ... the Koran refers to Musa Moses Karimullah, who spoke with God, and Jesus Masih Issa Ruhallah or the soul of God."

He was equally vocal in extolling the virtues of Saddam Hussein, saying that a balance was needed to correct the media picture of the Iraqi president as a Hitler and the "Butcher of Baghdad." He asked why nobody spoke about Hussein's policies that had virtually abolished illiteracy by threatening jail terms for parents who did not send their children to school, his massive construction of highways, bridges, and five-star hotels, or the new industries that had raised Iraq from a Third World economy to something far superior.

His views, of course, did not sit well with many. And as the countdown to the war neared and the media stories about domestic terrorism continued, unknown to himself, Thomas became someone to keep an eye on — a security question mark. In early January came the stories about Saddam Hussein threatening to use Muslim terrorists to strike out at coalition targets worldwide. The Toronto *Sun* published stories about a dozen Iraqi agents in the Toronto area waiting to strike at targets such as the Pickering reactor.

At about the same time, Thomas got a call from a man who gave his name as Andy Ellis. He was an official of the Canadian Security Intelligence Service. He wanted to come up to Ajax with his partner, Derek Huzulak, and interview Thomas in his home as part of the terrorism assessment that CSIS was doing. CSIS's job was to forestall any terrorist threat. And from their point of view, there was really only one man to check out at Pickering — Thomas.

Thomas said the CSIS official phoned him and said that because of the Gulf situation, there might be sabotage or some other action by local Iraqis and that CSIS was worried about Pickering. Thomas began protesting. "I said, 'If you mean me and my community, we are passive Christian people, we don't interfere, we don't have any political affiliation, and the majority are either here as refugees or to seek a good living. They are not out to go and cause sabotage, not our people. Who told you? The CIA?' The man was quiet and said he wanted to come and see me, and I said, 'No. Talk to me on the phone, and I'll talk to you.' "

Thomas was candid about his views on Iraq. He said that it was the country of the ten thousand Chaldeans in southern Ontario. Many of them were born there, their ancestors came from northern Iraq, they were the indigenous Iraqis. He told Ellis that the Chaldeans still love Iraq. "They are for Iraq, whether under Saddam or someone else. If we betray Iraq, then tomorrow I am going to betray Canada, I'll sell Canada to the highest bidder."

Thomas said he was furious as Ellis talked on about saboteurs, describing scenarios that the Iraqi had read in news accounts and watched on television. Thomas was never directly accused of being a terrorist, but the underlying accusation was implicit in all the questions CSIS posed. To begin with, why focus on Thomas? The Iraqi believed that the basis of the suspicion was his racial origin and media accounts of domestic terrorism. "It was in the media that ... there are ten or twelve Iraqis, and they are targeting nuclear stations. I am the commissioning engineer at the power plant; I was the engineer to commission Pickering. I have been there since day one. I commissioned the power plant up to the last unit. Do you think I would go and destroy something I built?" Thomas believes that his telephone was nevertheless tapped. Based on his engineering knowledge, he said he could easily interpret the sounds he heard on the line whenever he picked up the receiver.

He said Ellis was polite and questioned him for about an hour on the telephone, then left his telephone number and his pager number and bid him goodbye. Before hanging up, he told Thomas to call him if either he or any member of the Chaldean community had problems as a result of the war, and CSIS would look after it. Thomas did call him about Fares Yakow, the Iraqi high school student who was viciously beaten by a gang in Toronto. He said Ellis promised to go over and talk to the family and take care of the matter, but he never did.

Soon after Thomas's interview with Ellis, the bombardment of Baghdad began, and a new pall of gloom spread over the Iraqi community as all communications with Iraq — by letter or telephone — were cut off. When Thomas and Victoria heard reports about Basra in Southern Iraq, they were petrified. Thomas's brother was the Chaldean Archbishop of Basra, and Victoria had several immediate members of her family in that city. They watched the news of the bombardment in Ajax, helpless, unable to find out if the family members were alive or dead.

At work, Thomas found some of his co-workers actually very polite during the war. His boss, knowing Thomas's love for Iraq, called him in on the first day of the war and suggested that if he felt like it, he could take a few days off to get over the war strain. But simultaneously, with all the media publicity about terrorists, Ontario Hydro was part of a special meeting organized by the Ontario government to review security. However, the socialist government of Bob Rae made it clear that there would be no paranoia. Rae himself opposed the war, in keeping with the federal NDP stand.

All of a sudden, with the start of the war, Thomas noticed heightened security at the plant. As if aware of his sensitive feelings, his boss again called him in and asked him not to take this personally; it was not directed against him. A special memo on security had been issued to the employees, warning about possible terrorist attempts and asking them to be vigilant. In all such corporate memos, the unwritten line, of course, was that they should be vigilant against attacks by Arabs and Muslims. The entire plant was covered with security personnel. All cars travelling into the reactor were searched before entering, including those of all employees with the exception of one — the Iraqi engineer who had built the plant. Thomas had made it clear that he would take this as a personal affront, and "they did not dare to ask me to open my trunk."

But the war was beginning to take its toll on Thomas and a series of incidents accelerated the stress. First, there was the beating of Fares Yakow. Then Thomas came home one day to find that the mailbox at the entrance to his driveway had been smashed: this would be the first act of vandalism the Thomases had faced since they moved to the country home. Shortly after this, his youngest daughter, who works for a Canadian Tire store in the town of Bracebridge, came home with a tale. She works in the firearms department and handles the licensing required before hunting rifles can be purchased. She was processing a man's application and asked him casually, "Well, what are you going to hunt with this gun?" The man, a white Canadian, replied, "I'm going to hunt me some A-rabs." After this event, the tales of racial harassment in the workplace, at schools, on the streets became a flood.

It was thus in an angry mood that Thomas faced External Affairs Minister Joe Clark on January 28, 1991, at Toronto's Royal York Hotel. He was part of a delegation of Arabs put together by the Canadian Arab Federation. When Clark stood up to reassure the Arabs that they should not feel bad about the war or Canada's participation in it, since it was a United Nations' action, Thomas could not bear it any longer. He stood up and interrupted Clark: "Let me quote another prominent Canadian, Stephen Lewis, who was our former ambassador to the United Nations, who said that America had hijacked the U.N. They bribed Egypt by writing off $13 billion in loans, they bribed Syria, they even bribed China to go along with them. ... Your Operation Desert Shield [to protect Saudi Arabia from Iraq] turned into a Desert Storm, and Desert Storm turned into a genocide against Iraq and civilian areas got bombed. ... Yesterday, they bombed Sulaimanya, which, to begin with, is not even Arab; it is Kurd, and I know what is there, the only factory there is a cigarette factory. So what are you bombing there. ... Don't tell me about the U.N. You destroyed a Church, the Lady of Sorrow built eighteen hundred years ago. Its artefacts are older and more precious than the Sistine Chapel. You wiped that out in the Christian quarters. Within thirty miles of it there is no military installation. ... And we thought we were coming to a Christian country in Canada and would feel at home and welcome."

He went on about the racism that the Iraqis were facing, the interrogations by the RCMP and CSIS. James Kafieh, president of the CAF, said about Thomas's performance that it was "wonderful, Clark did not have a word to say." Thomas was questioning what he called the double standard in Canada. He said that while his people were beside themselves with anxiety about their relatives in Iraq, "when the first Scud missile fell on Israel, the government opened up a trunk telephone line, a 1-800 free line on government expense for the Jews to phone their relatives in Israel. I told Joe Clark about this and said, 'Why are you denying us the sending of a letter?' He did not say anything, this is what kills me, he wouldn't reply, and I was mad at him, I was shouting at him."

Surrounded by heavy security — from the RCMP and the Metro Toronto Police's VIP escort section — the minister left the meeting. He would comment and reply the next day in Ottawa at a meeting with five Muslim imams. He would tell them that the Royal York meeting was good catharsis for the Arabs.

Thomas had the right to be angry and disillusioned with Canada. Like many other Arabs and Muslims targeted by the security forces, he had given his best years to this country. His work record is impeccable, with nothing but diligence to mark his lengthy service with Ontario Hydro. And as for the issue of security, those employed by Hydro in key positions such as the one held by Thomas undergo extensive security checks that are routinely updated.

The decision to target Thomas seems racially motivated, since there is no record of CSIS or the other forces involved questioning the loyalty of similarly positioned employees at Pickering. No doubt, CSIS was also spurred by Thomas's views about the war, which may have been passed on by some overly imaginative fellow employee. But then, isn't such legitimate dissent what democracy is all about? If the force had hoped to mute Thomas's criticism, it failed. Thomas continued espousing the same opinions. He gave lengthy interviews to a national television network and to newspapers. But the Canadian whose loyalty had been rudely questioned found that few if any of his unpopular views made either the airwaves or the printed page.

CHAPTER EIGHT

The Symptoms of Fear

"To pronounce Mohammad is not all that difficult. But I have hardly met anybody who is willing to pronounce Mohammad right ... this society won't even make the attempt to pronounce our names."

Montreal psychiatrist Mohammad Amin

As the search for terrorists continued unabated, Canada's Arabs and Muslims began experiencing a crisis whose effects are rarely if ever tabulated in dollars and cents — the symptoms of mental trauma triggered by the massive bombing of largely Muslim Iraq. The mental anguish started with a feeling among Arabs and Muslims that they were isolated and alienated from the warlike goals of the Christian majority.

When the symptoms of anxiety and neurosis began to show, local Islamic associations in several cities began approaching experts, seeking help. In Montreal, more than fifty children were assembled for a group therapy session. They were encouraged to share their experiences with each other and with the professionals. The same approach was taken with adults, since in many cases it was their anxieties that had been picked up by their children.

The job of minding the mental health of the flock in Montreal fell on Dr. Mohammad Amin, a psychiatrist who divides his time between two hospitals. Yet he manages to save enough time to help the Muslim community of Quebec run its mosque. Dr. Amin's regular Muslim caseload increased by an incredible 2,000 per cent, and he encountered situations that almost reduced him to tears. He handled children and adults, Muslims and non-

Muslims, whites and people of colour. Sometimes, he would sit down at the end of the day and wonder if anybody in Ottawa had foreseen the human costs of the Gulf War on the home front.

Fifty-three-year-old Dr. Amin is full of energy. He is a little man, dark skinned, with thick glasses, and he can manage a friendly smile even as he describes some of the most traumatic cases. A Muslim from Bombay, he grew up on a famous street known as Mohammed Ali Road. During the day, the street is a jungle of cars and trucks and handcarts, a continuous din of people shouting, horns tooting, and the crash of goods being unloaded. The busy thoroughfare is lined with five- and six-storey buildings containing small flats crammed with people. The main levels of the buildings facing the street house everything from restaurants to bakeries and jewellers. After he had finished his schooling and university in that city, Dr. Amin's family decided he should leave and pursue his goals elsewhere. Muslims are by and large second-class citizens in India, and Dr. Amin was among thousands of Muslims who left India to seek a fairer deal elsewhere.

He spent two of the worst years of his life in Britain and has refused to go back to that country ever since. He had a scholarship to study there, but he gave it up because of the racism. His most vivid memory is hunting for a room to rent. He began going into corner stores, where people with such rooms would put up little notices. He was horrified to see that a majority of them had a postscript: "No coloureds, Irish or dogs." He then came to Canada but went on to study for two years in the United States with the idea of perhaps settling there. He found it only somewhat better than England and decided to move to Canada.

Given his experiences, he did not cherish the thought of living with anglos, as he calls English-speaking whites, and he settled in Montreal, doing some further studies at McGill University. And he is glad he did. "The French," he said, "are more willing to accept Muslims although we are told that the French are much more xenophobic. They may not like foreigners, but they don't have the hatred for foreigners like the English. The French may not associate with you, but they won't hate you." His observation would be proved right to some extent, for most of the racist backlash that the Muslims of Montreal suffered came from English-speaking Montrealers. The mosque itself is situated in an

English area, and racist graffiti were scribbled on its walls and
bags of excrement and garbage were flung at its entrance after the
war started. The Muslims found that the most negative articles
about the war were published in the English-language *Gazette*,
while the French press gave the issue a much more sympathetic
and objective treatment.

Dr. Amin found that the battle to stake out an equal place for
Muslims was still an uphill one, but he feels he stands a better
chance in Quebec than in English Canada. There are still battles
to be fought over the curriculum for the Islamic School, government grants, and teaching Islam to Muslim students in place of
Christianity, but he does not see these problems as insur-
mountable.

Historically, Quebec was also where the first Arab immigrants
landed just before the turn of the century, giving francophones a
longer exposure to Middle Easterners. And although the early
Arabs were mainly Christians, they were followed by scores of
Muslims. Most of them became peddlers who travelled the length
and breadth of Quebec, and some of their accounts reveal the
hospitality of the French, who would always let them stay over-
night when there was a heavy snowfall or the hour was late.

In contrast to this, W. D. Scott, Canada's superintendent of
immigration, stated in official correspondence in 1903 that the
Syrian peddlers (Arabs were largely classified as Syrian in those
days) were "more of a nuisance than anything else to the residents
of Canada." He acknowledged their ability to make money
through trade and real estate, but added that "there is, however, a
higher standard of citizenship than the mere ability to acquire
dollars and cents ... the Syrians are looked upon by the Department as undesirable immigrants."

Being in French Canada, though, did not make Dr. Amin's job
any easier during the Gulf War. For him, the war began right in
his practice. Within twenty-four hours of the bombs falling on
Baghdad, Muslim patients began calling for appointments. Prior
to the war, he saw one Muslim patient a month, at most. In the
first week of the war, he saw five people who had begun internal-
izing the conflict. He was shocked when this stream of patients
continued for the duration of the war, until February 28. Then,
almost as if by magic, they stopped showing up. But during the

war, his phone rang continually, with Muslim after Muslim seeking an appointment.

The cases were very specific to Islam and to the bombing of Iraq. For instance, one man forcibly brought to the hospital was the comptroller of a large investment bank. He was a man whom Dr. Amin describes as "a perfectly solid citizen, very much down to earth, being in the finance business." On the third day of the war, the man began to show signs of stress, and then he went "totally berserk to the point that he had to be admitted against his will." His extreme condition followed graphic reports of the devastating U.S. bombing raids on Baghdad.

At first, the man insisted that there was nothing wrong with him. He talked in fragmentary sentences that would have made little sense to someone without an Islamic background. The fragments included talk about Muslims being slaughtered, about sins, about Riba, or interest, about the five pillars of Islam — declaring every day that there is one God and Mohammed is his prophet, praying five times a day, fasting during Ramadan, giving a percentage of one's earnings to charity, and making a pilgrimage at least once to Mecca.

The key to his behaviour, Dr. Amin determined, was that he was blaming the deaths of the Muslims in Iraq on his own sinful ways, which included, for instance, charging interest on loans, which is banned in Islam. Other aspects of his personal life in the fast lane of finance also conflicted with the rules of Islam, and all of these conflicts surfaced in the context of the war. The man stayed up all night on the first day of the war, praying. He did the same on the second day and began to break down on the third. He continued to insist that there was nothing wrong with him. It would be a month before he began to realize what he had undergone, and the experience left him shattered.

Equally disturbing was another case that came Dr. Amin's way a week or so later. This one involved a twenty-year-old Lebanese Muslim woman. Again, her troubles began after hours of watching the crippling blow being dealt Iraq by the coalition aircraft. She not only internalized the conflict but also began to personalize it. In her twisted logic, she reasoned that Muslims were dying in the thousands because believers like her had committed sins and had done something grievously evil to cause this state of affairs to exist. Dr. Amin said: "She reasoned: 'I am a Muslim and I have done something wrong.' This is how the whole cycle starts. [Had Canada adopted a more neutral stand in the conflict] it would have made things easier because then, in opposing the war, you would have been part of the majority, then you would not have had the stress of being different from the rest."

As a result, late one evening, the Lebanese woman put on her hejab, ran out onto a main street, right in the middle of the road, and began asking passersby and passing motorists to forgive her for her sins so that the Muslim slaughter could be stopped.

Then there was the case of an eighteen-year-old Palestinian youth who had come to Montreal from Saudi Arabia in early 1990, to finish his education. As America and its allies began massing troops around Iraq and in Saudi Arabia, the youth was admitted to the emergency ward of the hospital. He was convinced that he was going to die very shortly. The hospital called Dr. Amin, and he took up the case. The youth visited Dr. Amin several times and was admitted to the emergency ward on at least five occasions. But his condition worsened during the war, and the doctor said he has no hesitation in blaming the war for the mental trauma the youth suffered.

The depression and panic attacks he endured prior to the war quadrupled. He became suspicious of everyone around him and began to avoid his friends at the pre-university course he was taking. He was convinced that they were all looking at him very oddly. He did not want to pray for fear of attracting attention as a Muslim. He became confused, unable to understand whether Canada was the right place for him or whether his parents and his brother were still alive in Saudi Arabia.

In this state of mind, he appeared for his examinations in March. Dr. Amin said he just sat in front of his papers and wrote nothing. Two months later, he wrote his examinations again, and this time he failed every subject — his first academic failure ever. Dr. Amin said that the young man's entire life had just crumbled around him and that it will take him years to pick up the pieces. "But this was just one of many similar cases. In fact, he told me about a friend of his who was undergoing the same symptoms and had promised to bring him along at the next session, but he never did."

But although Arabs and Muslims were more directly affected by the war, they were not the only ones. As the war dragged on,

Dr. Amin noticed that a wider section of the population was also beginning to be affected by the conflict. Close to the end of the war, the police brought a young French-Canadian man to Dr. Amin's hospital. He was white and, like the investment banker, had undergone a breakdown. He lived on a farm just outside Montreal, and everything seemed to be going well until the war started. For a time, there were some oddities in his behaviour and speech, but nothing extraordinary. However, his fear about the war continued to increase, as if the war was taking place right in Canada. And once Canadian aircraft joined in the offensive and there was some speculation in the media about Canadian land forces being sent over, the farmhand completely broke down.

One day, he suddenly became certain that Canada was about to commit large numbers of soldiers and would enforce conscription, just as it had in the Second World War. Still in his shorts, he ran out of the farmhouse and headed down the road to escape conscription. It was sub-zero weather. Luckily, his co-workers alerted police, who sent patrol cruisers out to locate him. He ran some five kilometres over roads and through the bush before police caught up with him. In his light clothing, it was a miracle that he survived.

Others from the white community were also affected. One English-speaking woman was brought to Dr. Amin. She was delirious and babbled incessantly about the war in the Middle East. "She claimed that she was a CIA agent who was in direct contact with George Bush and had the power to control the events and people, including Saddam Hussein. Tonight, she said, she had a special mission to perform, but she could not say what it was, at least not yet."

Another patient with a persecution complex had to be restrained from watching the television news by the staff of the Douglas Hospital Centre where Dr. Amin works. The man broke down when the war started and each newscast simply triggered and increased his symptoms.

"The point I am trying to make," says Mohammad Amin, "is that we do not pay attention to the cost to your psyche that comes out of this sort of event. And that is not restricted to Muslims; it happens to everybody."

Amin said that attributing a lot of this stress to the war alone would be simplistic and that there were other factors that added to the internalization of the conflict. Much of the blame he put on articles in newspapers and TV newscasts that portrayed Islam as a backward system that needs reform. In the media Muslims are portrayed either as "terrorists, oil sheikhs, or masters of a harem," he said. The fact that Islam is simply another branch of the tree from which Christianity and Judaism grew is never emphasized when the West talks about its Judeo-Christian heritage. As a result, Montreal's approximately thirty thousand Muslims are put in a very specific and negative mould that isolates them from the mainstream. Dr. Amin said other happenings during the war, such as talk in the community about selected Muslims being targeted by the RCMP and CSIS and the local forces, again reinforced the alienation among the Muslims, increasing their stress level.

Dr. Amin noted that when one considered the stresses of the war — the daily litany of TV pictures and biased stories, the racial incidents, the questioning of Arabs and Muslims — they all naturally heightened the paranoia among adults. "People become over careful about everything and everybody. They won't speak out their beliefs if the beliefs happen to be contrary to popular ones. They start feeling insecure about their environment, about themselves and their future."

Although the mental traumas he witnessed were at the extreme end of this anxiety spectrum, he could also see a change in people's everyday behaviour. For instance, the mosque had begun to have a closer liaison with the Jewish B'nai B'rith organization over the question of racism. Dr. Amin had delegated a Muslim to attend their meetings. He was stunned to find out from the minutes of the meeting that the man had refused to reveal his name and had deliberately said that he was Pakistani and not Arab. During the war he found a reluctance among people to attend meetings and demonstrations. He questioned the reluctant Muslims, and they told him that they did not want to be photographed, identified, and targeted; hence, they would rather suppress their beliefs than come out publicly. Many of the Muslims, Dr. Amin said, were Palestinians who had no homeland to go back to. They had come to Canada hoping to settle down, and now they were finding out that they might well face the same persecution here from the whites as they had from the Israelis.

In this situation, the most vulnerable were the children, who, in addition to picking up stress and anxiety from their elders, felt the urge to conform at school so that they would not be rejected by their peers. He first saw this in his own family. Dr. Amin and his wife have been married for twenty years, but they are childless, which explains the boundless energy he directs towards his sub-stitute family, the Muslim Ummah, or nation. He also spends a lot of time with his sister and her children. One evening, over supper, he noticed that his seven-year-old niece was very anxious about going to school. She was complaining about a stomachache. As a psychiatrist, he judged immediately that her symptoms related to a heightened level of stress. He began talking to her and soon found out what was bothering her.

At home and in the Muslim community, she was picking up some very specific messages: Dr. Amin believes that 90 per cent of Montreal's Muslims were against the war. The girl, who is in Grade 2, was also picking up the community's anxieties about the slaughter of Muslims at the hands of the Westerners. But in school, it was another story. Her teacher, who happened to be Jewish, talked about the evil Arabs, the Iraqi Scud missiles land-ing on Tel Aviv, and the gas masks that Israeli families had to sleep with. The talks by the teacher began turning the students against Iraq and against Arabs and Muslims. Most people still associate being Arab with being Muslim although about 18 per cent of Arabs are Christians.

Amin was shocked and insisted that his sister complain to the principal and the teacher right away about instilling this sort of hate in such young children. His sister refused, fearful of what would happen to her daughter if she did. He then said he would go and object, and his niece, equally fearful, asked him not to. "Fear is the one thing that has run through almost any person that I have come in contact with. For instance, if we organized a demonstration, few people would turn up, and when we asked them why, the standard answer was, 'We did not want to be photographed by the police or CSIS.' That fear is actually very deep, and my assessment is that we are treated as outsiders in this country, and somehow, and this is where I am very angry at ourselves, we have fallen into this trap. We consider ourselves as outsiders, as guests, rather than as equal partners in this country."

With children, he said, the fear of rejection is even greater. His niece continually worried about rejection by her classmates, who all backed the coalition and Israel. He said that for a Muslim child, the fear is exacerbated because they are named Ahmed or Mohammed rather than Bill or Bob, which singles them out immediately. Moreover, he said, the non-Muslim children and adults do not make any effort to understand their culture; they do not even learn how to pronounce their names. He cited the example of George Bush, who consistently mispronounced Saddam Hussein's name. "The Week in Review," a show produced by the Public Broadcasting System in the United States, noted that Bush had learned to pronounce his foe's name properly only after the war had ended. Much effort now goes into pronouncing difficult Russian and Polish names correctly, Amin pointed out. Surely the same could be managed for Arabs and Muslims.

In addition to aches, pains, and recurring nightmares, children display other symptoms when their stress and anxiety levels increase, Dr. Amin said. He found these symptoms showed up in their day-to-day activities in class and in the playground. Among other things, Arab and Muslim children became less attentive in class and more easily distracted. In the playground, they were more irritable, which translated into short tempers, arguments, and even fist fights. Such insecurity, he said, also meant the child might withdraw from regular friends and try to secure his or her place in isolation at home.

"Racial taunting was the most obvious cause of all this," he said. "And we saw much of that, although a regular pattern as in other cities was missing. What all this adds up to is a decline in the child's level of confidence. Once you begin to question who you are and where you are … am I really a Canadian? Will I be allowed to remain in Canada? … then you are looking at all kinds of problems. And what I am telling you is not specific to Montreal. I can guarantee that the effects can be extrapolated and applied to Muslim children in general across the country."

The Montreal community runs Sunday classes for its children at the mosque. And after parents reported the trauma the children were going through with the consistent name-calling, which was showing up in other forms of disorder, such as a loss of appetite and lack of sleep, it was decided to hold a group session. The children were asked to relate their experiences to each other and to describe various coping techniques. In this way they could find solace in the fact that others around them were experiencing similar problems. A session was also held for the parents, many of whom were suffering from anxiety themselves and then had to deal with the anxieties of their children. In addition, the mosque had faced acts of desecration by vandals. Even newspaper photographers and TV cameramen making an appearance at the mosque set off alarm bells among the children, who started to see themselves as some sort of strange breed, different from other children.

But Montreal is a large cosmopolitan city with people from many different cultures. In smaller cities, such as those in Western Canada, the impact on children was greater. There are about three thousand Muslims in the entire province of Manitoba, most of them concentrated in its capital city of Winnipeg. The Manitoba Islamic Association helped two Muslim psychologists to arrange a group therapy session for about thirty children. The session revealed some alarming problems. One of the sadder cases was that of an eight-year-old boy who had a recurring nightmare of a white man chasing him with a gun, often getting close enough to shoot and kill him. As the other children listened, the boy described the chase and how, at the crucial moment, it was too terrifying and he woke up. The boy shook nervously as he narrated the dream. Like the others, the young boy said he could not talk to his parents about the dream because they were already very upset about the war.

The children did not feel close enough to their teachers or guidance counsellors to approach them on the issue of the war and how it affected Muslims. The association decided to go public, and an enterprising reporter at the *Winnipeg Free Press* wrote a front-page story about the impact of the war on Muslim children. Almost immediately, the school board reacted with concern, said Khalid Iqbal, head of the association, and began taking special measures to help the Muslim students.

The Canadian government, its security forces, and, in some cases, the media, all subtly implied that the country's Arabs and Muslims were not to be trusted, that they were the "enemy" and the potential terrorists. As a result of having their loyalties questioned, many Arabs and Muslims developed symptoms of anxiety and paranoia. Arabs and Muslims in Montreal were lucky to have Dr. Amin, a psychiatrist who brought a cultural understanding to his therapy. But he was convinced that the cases he handled were only the tip of the iceberg. Similar cases were reported from Winnipeg and Halifax.

The irony is that Arabs and Muslims who are loyal to Canada and who belong to Canadian society became the victims of the foreign-policy decisions of a government which decided to wage war against a foreign state thousands of kilometres away. The Gulf War had more than just one front, and it was the Gulf War within Canada whose victims Mohammad Amin tried to help.

CHAPTER NINE

Staking the Mosques

"The mosque compared to other religious institutions has the least objects in it, you go in and what is there? Nothing. But you can go into a mosque to hide from society. Some people go to bars, we go to a mosque. Why would the security forces target mosques?"

Montreal economist and Muslim activist
Amer Al-Roubaie

During the war, when Muslims were the targets of Canada's security forces, attention was concentrated on their places of worship, the mosques, and on the Muslim equivalent of active church members. These activists are usually considered benign volunteer workers who help make sure that the church functions smoothly. During the Gulf War, however, they were regarded as potential terrorists.

In Montreal, CSIS and the Mounties targeted nine mosques, among them one run by the Muslim Community of Quebec because of its large and politically active congregation. For the MCQ, such targeting was not new. The mosque president had once been shown a file folder by the Quebec government's intelligence service. The folder was full of photographs of parishioners whom the service wanted identified.

During the Gulf War, CSIS decided to target an Iraqi Canadian named Amer Al-Roubaie, an economist and secretary of the mosque committee. Al-Roubaie had earlier laughed off a warning from a colleague that he would likely be questioned. The warning came after a supper at the colleague's home, when the other man saw a car pull up behind Al-Roubaie's car as the economist left for home.

Al-Roubaie is a small, soft-spoken academic who lives by himself near the mosque and close to Concordia University's Loyola Campus. He has Ph.D. in economics, having completed his thesis on Third World development at McGill University. Each morning, he heads to McGill, mingling with professors, taking on the odd teaching assignment, or spending time in the library doing research for whatever freelance project he has accepted. Although his income is small, it is sufficient for his purposes. He is forty-five years old and a bachelor, which gives him time to spend his afternoons and evenings at the mosque, helping new immigrants or refugees with their paperwork, organizing the MCQ's office, and even undertaking such tasks as fixing the leaking roof.

He is a devout Muslim, but hardly a fanatic: he still attends evening functions with academics at the university and has no hesitation in saying that although he does not regularly drink alcohol or smoke, he may well end up sipping a beer at these parties. Al-Roubaie is probably one of the more popular and respected parishioners at the mosque.

What singles him out is his immense knowledge of Canada and his love for the country — the only one he has known since he left his native Iraq about twenty years ago. When he came here to specialize in economics, he had no desire to settle in Canada because his family is quite well off, with large farmlands on which tenant farmers grow pineapples, grapes, and oranges. But as time went on, and as he moved from university to university and city to city, he soon found himself settled to the point where Iraq became a distant memory. He returned for a visit only once in the early eighties.

Al-Roubaie first came to Fredericton, New Brunswick, a place that he still remembers and often visits. When he arrived, he did not speak a word of English, only Arabic. But that did not stall his academic ambitions. In two years, he was fluent in English. He finished his basic degree there, then moved to Carleton University in Ottawa, before being recommended to McGill for his Ph.D. In the twenty years that he has been here, he has devoted a lot of time to both national politics and the politics and the economics of various Canadian regions, familiarizing himself with the names of local politicians and following their exploits. He travelled a great deal and made fast friends in different parts of Canada from Halifax to Vancouver. After he had immersed himself thoroughly in Canada, it did not make sense, he said, to just pull up stakes and return home; he had become a full-fledged Canadian and got his citizenship in 1985. Besides, unlike other immigrants, his Canadian pursuits were not economically motivated — his father had enough retirement money saved up, and his brothers all had good jobs.

What attracted him most as a student of economic development was the multicultural nature of Canada, where he could meet people from all over the world, especially the Third World, and learn about their experiences and their homelands. He never did settle down in a teaching job or make a lot of money. "You may say I did not achieve much financially, but that is not my main concern in life at all. Things went fine. I travelled a lot, went to the best places in this country, compared to other people here, even native-born Canadians. People here need a lot of money to drive fancy cars, go to the Bahamas. Not me."

Instead, he has a network of friends spread over North America. If he needs money, they help out. He can travel and visit them for a month or two at a time. Similarly, when they come to Montreal, he moves in with a friend and lets them and their families use his one-bedroom apartment. Having friends such as these is better than an insurance policy, he believes.

In all this time, other than his one three-week visit home, his only connection with Iraq was with its consulate, for about five years between 1979 and 1984, when he worked part-time as an economist and public relations consultant for the Iraqi mission. If the consulate needed help in finding apartments for visitors or in writing letters to government officials or the media or in preparing other publicity material, he would help out. In 1984, when the Iraqis shut down their Montreal consulate, his association with the government of Iraq ended.

Shortly before Christmas, 1990, while the United Nations countdown to war was going on, Al-Roubaie came home one day and found a message on his answering machine. It was a man, who left his name and said he would call again. The next morning, he called and introduced himself. He was from CSIS. He asked Al-Roubaie what he did for a living, and when the Iraqi Canadian said he was an economist at McGill, the man from CSIS replied: "Oh yes, then you're the person I am after."

He asked Al-Roubaie whether they could get together that day so the economist could answer a few questions. The agent offered to come to his apartment or to meet him at the CSIS office. Al-Roubaie said that since he had to go to the vicinity of the CSIS office to pick up some mail, he would to drop in. He was apprehensive and nervous as he headed downtown. Different questions went through his mind: Why would the spy service seek him out? How much information did they have on him and why? He had done nothing wrong, he was never involved with the police before this, and the meeting would be his first contact in Canada with any kind of a police or security organization. Police and security, the Mukhabarat, are not happy associations for any Middle Easterner.

The interview lasted about an hour. The agent produced several pictures of local and other Arabs and asked Al-Roubaie whether he recognized any of them. Two of them were Iraqi consular officials whom he knew, and he said so. The agent then wanted to know about other Iraqis in Montreal, and although he did not use the word terrorist, it soon became obvious what he was after. Al-Roubaie made it clear that the Iraqi community numbers less than five thousand in Montreal and is almost entirely a refugee one, made up of people who had either run away from Saddam Hussein or left because of the Iran-Iraq war. "They won't get involved in any violence or sabotage, if that's what you're after," he told the agent.

But there were other set questions to answer. The agent wanted to know how Al-Roubaie felt about Canada being part of a war in the Middle East. Then the agent asked whether he supported Saddam Hussein. Al-Roubaie said he was shocked at that question because he had been so cut off from the internal politics of Iraq. "I told him that I could probably give him a better answer if he asked me whether I supported Brian Mulroney because the only contact I have left with Iraq is my family there, I've been here for so long."

About half an hour into the conversation, the agent himself began to get bored with the line of questioning. Apparently, Al-Roubaie, a full-fledged academic who was flying to Washington the following week to deliver a paper on Third World development, was not the agent's idea of a potential terrorist.

He began discussing economics with Al-Roubaie — the agent himself was a frustrated economist. He had studied at Carleton University in Ottawa and then at Queen's University in Kingston. That subject, of course, touched Al-Roubaie's first love, and they got involved in discussing various economic theories for the next half hour — terrorism, the Iraqi community, and Arabs all seemed to have vanished suddenly. When Al-Roubaie left the building, he stopped for a moment and began to wonder why he had been targeted in the first place. It did not seem to make sense. As he walked back to McGill, he thought about the agent's face, and he knew he had seen the man at the university, in the library and at other lectures and gatherings. He was the academic "spy" detailed to keep a tab on foreign students and professors whom Canada lets in but then has second thoughts about.

He recalled that the agent was at a loss to explain his targeting when Al-Roubaie questioned him in return. "I explained to him that I did not even have a traffic ticket in all my life in this country, I do not have any criminal record, I never had any problems, I travelled this country one end to the other. I have friends in every province of this country, and I have learned so much about its politics, the culture, about the linguistics, about the diversity, about so many other Canadian issues. But he did not have any answer to these types of thing. The Middle East is in turmoil, and there will be more problems there from time to time, and it is disheartening to know that whenever there is a problem over there, you will be the first victim here. I did not end up feeling really comfortable. That is the sad side of this whole issue."

He did not think it was just because he was an Iraqi that he was on CSIS's target list; it was also because he was an activist at the mosque, its secretary, familiar with the parishioners, friends with the Muslims in Montreal. He believes, given several other people who were approached and the types of questions directed at them, that there was a pattern of targeting devout Muslims and activists at their mosques. He believes there is concern in Canada about the spreading Muslim faith. There are about three hundred thousand Muslims in Canada, and their numbers are growing; the next census is expected to place them ahead of the Jews.

For a while, Al-Roubaie thought of leaving Canada and returning to Iraq. He did not think the much vaunted Charter of Rights
and Freedoms made sense after what he had gone through. Would
he ever be accepted as a Canadian? Wasn't it better to face the
primitive security services of Iraq and some other Third World
countries rather than the technologically superior one of the West,
where even if the spies did not talk to you, they knew your life
history through telephone taps, opening mail, and details from
other data banks. He believes, with some justification, that given
their superiority in information-gathering and spying techniques,
modern societies such as Canada are *ipso facto* police states —
they don't need to follow you; you are always under their watchful
eyes.

He was sad and angry, but then another realization came over
him. Although Ottawa had disappointed him, the province of
Quebec treated him well. Why should he consider himself a
Canadian? And so, in our second and last interview, as we chatted
casually over a Greek dinner, he commented: "You know what?
I've decided, I am not going to be a Canadian. Since I've spent
most of my years in Montreal, henceforth I am a Québécois. In
fact, I like the French! We have asked the province for a grant to
teach the Muslims at the mosque French. They will all be Québécois!"

CSIS had concluded in its continuing assessment of the war
situation that the threat of a terrorist incident in Canada was
remote. Moreover, the RCMP was coming up empty handed as it
conducted interview after interview. One would have thought that
after a week or so, such targeting would have died out, unless, of
course, it was motivated by more than information-gathering.
Perhaps the security forces were taking their cue from their political masters and the bureaucrats, especially from the Department
of External Affairs, which was at the centre of policy-making
during the conflict.

Evidence suggests that this was the case. Shortly after the
invasion of Kuwait, the federal minister of housing, Alan Redway,
who has many Muslims and Arabs in his riding, sought a meeting
between External Affairs Minister Joe Clark and six Muslim
imams who had specific concerns. He found Clark receptive, but
the mandarins in External Affairs were opposed to such a meeting.

They continued to block it, arguing that "it would cause undefined problems."

Eventually, Clark met Imams Said Zafar, Ezz Gad, Abdullah Hakim, Abdul Hameed Gabier, Ahmad Kutti, and Abdul Mohsin Jamil on January 30 for about forty-five minutes. The imams were concerned about the Muslim image in Canada and sought the appointment of Muslims in External Affairs, especially as ambassadors, in order to educate Canadians about Islam.

Clark was blunt. He said he would not appoint a Muslim as an ambassador to a Muslim country. Who would the ambassador be loyal to, Islam or Canada? His top bureaucrats listened quietly, and Clark did not elaborate. The bias in the statement was clear. Would he apply the same rule when appointing Christians to a Christian country or Jews to Israel? If the job of an ambassador is to create goodwill and, presumably, trade links, then what better way than to show the multiracial character of Canada?

A day later, Redway wrote a personal and confidential letter to Clark. The following portions are worth noting:

> I am sure that you have sensed from previous communications, meetings and discussions, the deep distrust that Canadians of Muslim origin have for our government. They feel that both their political representatives and the bureaucracy are strongly prejudiced against them, even though many of them are third and perhaps fourth generation Canadians. ... You and I both know that this is ... not government policy. It may very well be the policy of the bureaucracy to treat Canadian Muslims as second-class citizens, but it is not the policy of the Mulroney government ... I hope that you will correct this impression.

Clark never did.

Al-Roubaie's experiences, like those of other Muslims interviewed for this book, suggest that during the Gulf War our security forces often targeted individuals based on their race and religion. While white Canadians could speak out against the war, if Arabs and Muslims opposed it, they became potential saboteurs

The Gulf Within

and terrorists in the eyes of the security forces. Certainly, nothing in Al-Roubaie's background save his race and his religious activism at the local mosque explains the decision to target him. Traditionally, security forces take their marching orders from their political masters. When high-ranking ministers, such as Joe Clark, question whether Muslims can be loyal to Canada as well as Islam, then it is no surprise that CSIS should target Al-Roubaie. Clark's comments, and the anti-Muslim bias displayed by university-trained senior bureaucrats in External Affairs, strengthen the conclusion that security targeting during the war was racially motivated.

Part II

CHAPTER TEN

When CSIS Calls

"One can't codify the laws of intelligence and espionage. They are necessarily passionate and extra rational, like love letters."

CSIS Director Reid Morden in a 1989 speech, quoting the right-wing American columnist William F. Buckley

A national security operation of the kind launched by the RCMP and CSIS during the Gulf War requires three prerequisites to ensure success: a co-operative media, political backing, and unsophisticated targets. The two agencies were blessed with all three. Perhaps the easiest of the three was the media, one police officer said in a candid conversation. The media had new technology to write about, new buzzwords to explain, the villains and convoluted politics of the Middle East to discuss. It was a matter of getting a chain reaction going and then letting media competition take over. Politicians could have reined in the Mounties and CSIS, but they wouldn't when bureaucrats quietly informed them that they would have to face the people if, in fact, something did happen. And the targets? They were mostly new Canadians; they were hardly likely to protest and lobby.

During the operation, the public front put forward by the agencies was one of calm and composure. CSIS, for instance, would point out that its agents were behaving like reporters — simply knocking on doors and holding polite conversations. Yet another agency, Canada Customs, which does the initial immigration checks at points of entry, had perhaps the best excuse for some of its excesses. It minded the doors Arab terrorists could sneak in, and hence it had to be even more vigilant.

However, when one breaks down the security operation into its components and examines each aspect separately, the scenario is frightening — and ought to make Canadians sit up and rethink whether Canada's involvement in the war was worth the human costs.

CSIS had a dual role. On the one hand, it was to provide a risk assessment to the government, based on its interviews with Arab, mostly Iraqi, Canadians. In its other role, it was to target suspects. But in a majority of its public statements it stressed assessment, painting a picture of benign agents telephoning in advance like encyclopedia salespeople and offering multiple choices of times and venues or visiting homes after supper during the quiet hour and politely requesting information to help Canada. Based on these interviews and on information its own people were sending from the Middle East embassies where they are stationed, it provided regular assessments to the government.

Arabs were nevertheless angry at these interviews, even though CSIS spokesman Gerry Cummings defended the method, turning the table on the Arabs. "Are they Canadians?" he asked. "They have said that they owe their allegiance to Canada. They've been here for a long time. It is a possibility that they can help this country in a time of stress, and a very open, legal, legitimate representative of the government of Canada comes and asks you some questions about violence within this country. Is that oppression? Is that intimidating?"

In fact, the interviews were not as benign as Cummings and CSIS Director Reid Morden made them out to be. If all CSIS wanted to know was whether the respondents believed something would happen in Canada, it could have commissioned Gallup to do a weekly survey. But CSIS was after more than just this information. It had targeted Arabs and Muslims, and it wanted to know about their political beliefs. It wanted to fathom the amount of support for the Gulf War, not among the people at large, but among a distinct racial and religious group — Arabs and Muslims. Canada's constitution garantees citizens and residents the freedom of expression and belief, so the RCMP and CSIS interviews did not violate any law. When a police officer arrests a person, the law is very clear. The officer must have "reasonable and probable grounds," or what the Americans call "just cause," to do so. The officer cannot arrest someone on the basis of a vague suspicion. But there is no law controlling when and under what circumstances officers can show up at someone's doorstep to talk to him or her. The law gives individuals the right to refuse to talk, but experience shows that the authority surrounding police officers overwhelms even the bravest. Arabs subjected to RCMP or CSIS questioning often stated, "I agreed to talk because I didn't want the police to think that I was guilty of something." For Canadians of Third World origin, the presence of a police officer or security agent is intimidating. And discussing politics with Mounties or CSIS agents — even though the latter are not police officers and have no power to arrest — is not like discussing politics with a group of friends. One officer asks questions, and the other makes notes. Those who experienced this questioning during the war found it unnerving. Consider the interview of an Iraqi-born research technologist who lives in Vancouver. He is a Canadian citizen and has been in the country for seven years.

The man, who requested anonymity, has patents on certain types of lithium batteries and works for a company that at one time was contracted to supply these products to the federal government. In the past he also worked for the American National Aeronautics and Space Administration (NASA), providing lithium batteries that were utilized in space craft. Two CSIS agents showed up at his home one Friday evening, unannounced. They were curt and rude, he said. "They showed me their badges and asked me if I was of Iraqi origin. When I said yes, they wanted to come in and talk to me. I said, 'No, you don't have a warrant to come in.' They insisted. ... I said, 'Give me your cards, and I'll call you on Monday.' They refused, and I said, 'Okay, in which case I can't call you.' Finally, they gave me their cards, and then one of them warned me, 'If you don't call us on Monday, we'll be here at your house on Tuesday evening.' That was threatening, it wasn't a request."

The physicist set up an interview at work. When CSIS arrived, his boss was in the room along with the head of the company's security. The physicist taped the interview and provided this author with a copy of the tape.

The agents began by asking whether he was a Shia or a Sunni Muslim, and when he said he was just a Muslim, they insisted on knowing which denomination.

Here are some of the other questions:

> *Since we have a war going on in the Gulf, I would like to solicit your general view of the war and Canada's involvement and the United States' involvement.*
>
> *Do you support the government of Saddam Hussein?*
>
> *How do you feel about Canada's role in participating? In that it is your homeland and the place of your birth? Do you think that Canada should have avoided playing a role in the war?*
>
> *Part of our responsibilities and duties is to do with terrorism and prevention of terrorism. So when we are at war with another country, we solicit the views of communities and people who are born or related to the general area of the Middle East. It is an ongoing thing as well, but it is particularly heightened at this particular junction in time. Because of that, I ask you about your feelings in regard to the war. And when you were in Iraq, did you ever belong to a political party? Were you a member of the Ba'ath Party [of Saddam Hussein] at any time?*
>
> *Did you ever involve yourself in any activities, or were you ever a member of any group opposing the government of the Ba'ath party. Or the Al Dawa party [a Shia opposition group in Iraq]? Are you familiar with that organization? What does that organization mean to you?*
>
> *Did you ever travel to Iran?*

Do you practise your faith? So you worship ... I don't
mean practise as just believe ... you practise and you
attend prayers? You do attend services?

We have a variety of mosques, masjids, here in Van-
couver. There is one on 99, there is one on Sexsmith
Street in Richmond, there is one in Burnaby. There is
a masjid in the 1400 block of Nanaimo. Where do you
attend? Is there any one of them you favour?

The interview was unconscionable. It was tantamount to intimidation, invasion of privacy, and a violation of the man's rights
under the Canadian Constitution. Right at the outset, for instance,
the two agents are heard on the tape announcing that they had
offered to interview the Iraqi in private but that he chose to have
the other two in the room. Is it agreed, one of the agents says, that
if at any time Mr. J chooses to reply in private that the other two
will leave the room? They clearly imply that at any time their
interview might lead to some sinister topic such as terrorism.

On the aspect of terrorism, question four is very cleverly
worded. If we strip away the garnish surrounding the question, we
are left with: "Part of our responsibilities and duties is to do with
terrorism and prevention of terrorism. ... *Because of that*, I ask
you about your feelings in regard to the war." The implication is
clearly that CSIS does suspect the Iraqi of being a potential terrorist.

For the state to inquire into and record the political and religious beliefs of one of its citizens is itself an Orwellian horror.
These two agents were doing the very thing that Canadians have
condemned in the past when discussing totalitarian regimes.
While the physicist was not overtly threatened during the interview, he was nevertheless unnerved by it. When a security organization evinces a particular interest in the beliefs of a citizen, the
effect is inevitably intimidating.

And what was it that this person was involved in? He was not
part of any Iraqi political movement in Canada. His only activity
was similar to that of Amer al-Roubaie in Montreal. He was part
of an Islamic theological study group in Vancouver, which dis-

cussed religious issues to bridge the gap between the different
Islamic sects. The group was attached to a local mosque, it was
not secretive, and its open aim was to set up a group known as
the United Muslim Association or UMA to end the schisms. CSIS
must have interviewed the handful of other people in the study
circle, which quickly broke up once the war started.

And what was the reason for the invasion of this Canadian's
privacy? The agents said that their security concern was aroused
by the fact that the company was a defence contractor for Ottawa.
When the boss remarked that the company had long since been
sold to a Japanese firm and was not involved in defence con-
tracting, the agents quickly suggested other reasons for the inter-
rogation — among them, that they wanted to know the physicist's
personal views about the war. His reply was very noncommittal
— to ensure that he was not persecuted because of his views.

The agents said they might want to come again. The technologist did not want them to return and told them that the reason he
had spoken to them was that he had nothing to hide. He had been
afraid that if did not submit to the interview, he might lose his job.
CSIS was at an advantage here, and it knew it. Had he refused to
be interviewed, they could have interviewed his boss about him,
in the process leaving the impression that there was some security
concern about the man.

Perhaps the most questionable statement from the agents came
after the technologist told them that the next time they should
phone ahead of time and "bring a warrant or something, I haven't
done anything and why should I be investigated?" One of the two
replied: "In a democracy ... we have the right to come and ask
you [questions] and talk to you."

But was there a real and tangible threat of terrorism? Strangely
enough, the assessments that CSIS did from September to the end
of the war on February 28 all indicated little or no threat. This
low-risk assessment continued even after Saddam Hussein was
quoted in the media asking Muslims the world over to strike at
coalition targets. The assessments were also distributed to the
RCMP, local police forces, and Customs and Immigration.

This raises several questions: Why were these assessments not
made public boldly and only referred to as asides in the debates
of the Commons' external affairs committee? Why was the media
not requested to stop their search for terrorists in view of this

low-risk assessment? Why was the RCMP unleashed with full force, utilizing its National Emergency Security Plan, which had never been used to this extent before? Why did prominent leaders, such as the prime minister and the solicitor general, speak from both sides of their mouths — there is a threat, but there is no imminent threat, but Canadians should be vigilant — creating a public paranoia that only fed the security apparatus? And more importantly, if there was no threat, why did CSIS itself continue to target people?

CSIS launched what Arabs like Rashad Saleh, former head of the Canadian Arab Federation, believe was one of the most pervasive and intensive security sweeps ever launched in Canada. "We've been going through many wars, in 1967, 1973, 1982 in Lebanon, but we never went through this kind of treatment," he said. "I've got feedback from Iraqis, Palestinians, Egyptians, Jordanians, you name it. We had at one point some thirty complaints, including from cities like Burlington, Oakville, and Ajax. Those are cases known to us. In each case those people were asked about three to five others by the security forces, so you can imagine the number."

It reached a point where James Kafieh, the president of CAF, published hundreds of brochures titled *When CSIS Calls*. The brochures listed the rights of Arab Canadians, including the right to refuse to talk to CSIS. They informed Arabs that they could in addition choose the place of meeting, have other people or lawyers with them, or ask CAF for assistance. Local Arabs groups were given this brochure, and they reproduced it in the hundreds.

The secrecy of the security operation blinded both the media and ordinary Canadians and got the full backing of Ottawa. It was done so quietly, and so swiftly, and left such a chilling effect that although hundreds of Arab Canadians were interrogated in their homes and offices, just a fraction called CAF to complain — and few of those complaints were of a nature that could be explained to the media in a way that would elicit a news story. In fact, most were either ignored by the media — they would require too much effort to dig out — or written up like the protestations and claims of a criminal being given his day in print.

CSIS Director Reid Morden, who refused to be interviewed for this book, acknowledged before the external affairs committee of Parliament that the feeling in the Arab community about CSIS interviews was so intense that the community was accusing the service and the RCMP of stifling free expression through intimidation. Svend Robinson, the champion of the Arabs and Muslims during the war, jumped in after this acknowledgement and asked the CSIS head to elaborate on how targets were picked. "Are all Iraqi Canadians who still have relatives in Iraq the subject of questioning? Are other Arab Canadians who have relatives in other countries in the Arab world, in the Muslim world, also considered fair game for questioning by CSIS? What are the ground rules for questioning in these circumstances?" Morden dodged the question, saying the MP could hardly expect him to outline their operational methods. He then tried to change the topic by talking of CSIS helping to prevent Iraqi spies from blackmailing Iraqi Canadians. Robinson kept on with his pursuit and demanded to know the reasoning used before CSIS agents went knocking on doors. He also wanted to know how many Arabs and Muslims had been interviewed, a question to which he would not get a reply.

CSIS's Gerry Cummings later said they interviewed about two hundred people, which, he believes, is next to nothing given that there are more than two hundred and fifty thousand Arabs in Canada. James Kafieh of CAF believes, based on a formula utilized by the Ontario Human Rights Commission, that for every complainant there are about five who do not bother to complain and therefore that the interview subjects numbered somewhere between five hundred and one thousand.

And then there was the photography. Both James Kafieh and Rashad Saleh had numerous complaints about Arabs being visited and shown photographs of others. In some cases, the photographs were taken at peace demonstrations. Among others, Professor Harish Jain, co-chair of Hamilton's anti-racism group, heard several such complaints. "The war was a nightmare for Arab groups in terms of intolerance, and on top of that you have this kind of harassment. What are we living in, a dictatorship? These are people who ran away from countries that have this sort of thing, and they come here to face the same thing, you have CSIS and other agencies investigating you and asking questions they have no right to ask. It was that kind of thing that was going on, the line of questioning was very wrong."

Gerry Cummings was emphatic that CSIS did not target peace rallies and considered them legitimate dissent. And he insisted that just because people were interviewed, it did not mean there was a file on them. So far, so good, but under questioning he acknowledged other facts. For instance, what if a so-called legitimate target attended a peace rally? "If any individual who is our target attends a rally, we would be interested in knowing who he or she is mixing with, not the rally." In this case, the gloves would come off, and that portion of the rally showing the contacts would be photographed. And after that, the targets would multiply — they would now include the people the first target was in touch with to determine their relationship with the original.

When Cummings was asked about the filing of information on people interviewed, he denied that this was done in the sense of creating a file on the individual person. Nevertheless, information is input and cross-referenced on databases, and the information would include the name of the person interviewed. According to CSIS insiders, after this an entry could simply be made seeking all references to a person, and all the cross-referenced material would show up. In the case of the Vancouver technologist hounded by CSIS, it would even show which mosque he attends and how faithfully he follows Islam.

The scariest part of the security sweep was the targeting of people and the methods that were used to persuade them to talk. The RCMP were better at this, perhaps because Mounties are policemen with the power to arrest, while CSIS agents are civilians. The RCMP pulled out all the stops and implemented the National Emergency Operations Plan. Inspector Robert Norton was in charge of the implementation and co-ordination in Ottawa. The Mounties, he said, are forbidden to investigate groups, which is left to CSIS. They only investigate individuals and individual threats.

"We would receive information that an individual was planning to get together money and explosives to do something. If that individual happened to be an Arab, so be it. We would investigate that individual." "How would they get the tips?" he was asked. "We would get telephone calls; there would be citizens who approached the police and said they were aware of something or somebody. It would then be handled by the National Security

Intelligence [Service]. We had a normal relationship with the FBI, and we got information from them, usually specific names."

But the majority of calls were from citizens, and these people put so much pressure on the Mounties that headquarters in Ottawa began to draft officers from other units, beginning with the Passport and Immigration section. Inspector Norton said officers worked tremendous overtime. They would be going off work, he said, and an anonymous call would come in, and it would have to be checked out. Since Canada was at war, tips were not screened; they were all investigated with equal zeal. According to a Metro Toronto Police officer who was involved with the RCMP, it reached the point where one could call in about a neighbour one did not like and the family would come under police scrutiny.

Inspector Norton said the most common kind of tip was somebody calling in and saying he knew so and so was planning a terrorist act. In most such cases, he said, the lead amounted to nothing, but it had to be checked out. He said there were literally hundreds of such calls — he lost count — all of which were checked out. He said he is not looking forward to the overtime bills when they come in.

Some of the leads that were investigated seem questionable. Majdi Hanoneh, a twenty-six-year-old Palestinian, who was himself interviewed by CSIS about a non-profit club he had set up, tells the following story. His uncle owns and operates a donut shop in Thornhill, a Toronto suburb. One day in the first week of the war the shopowner noticed two men who had coffee, paid, and left. An hour later, with the donut shop more than half full, they were back. This time, they approached the owner and flashed their badges. They were Mounties investigating a complaint that he "may be a threat to the security of Canada." When he asked them to elaborate on the complaint, one of them replied that a couple of customers had called the RCMP to say that they were at the donut shop a day earlier and had heard "a group of Arabs involved in lengthy discussions" relating to the war and that they felt the group was planning something. The uncle replied with a smile that since the first week of the war was barely underway, he would be surprised if his Arab customers did not discuss the war; everybody else did.

The Mounties then demanded the owner's identification — which is clearly a breach of his rights since he had not been charged with any offence. He protested. He was angry because his customers were watching and listening to the conversation. They had watched the two men flash their badges and talk of security and terrorism. He warned them toward the end that what they had done was bad for the store and for his business and that this sort of harassment had never happened to him in his twelve years in Canada. The two then left. Inspector Norton said they probably knew more than they were willing to let on and were waiting for a response — which never came.

Rashad Saleh said similar incidents took place at two Arab restaurants in Burlington, where business started dropping after the visits and the general tone of reports in the media. In Cambridge, Ontario, a Palestinian who owns several auto businesses and is very well placed financially was called up by a business associate of his, who told him that the Mounties thought he was a terrorist. The RCMP had been inquiring about his cash flow and the source of his funds. They were approaching his bankers and others he had dealt with, but they never came to him.

This type of *modus operandi* shows the Mounties were themselves under pressure to keep the flow of information continuing steadily. Every morning, Inspector Norton and his group would issue a summary of events that would go to the solicitor general and to the executive level of government, especially the cabinet security committee. The extensive nature of this summary gave the government a basis for announcing that the security forces had everything under control but that nevertheless vigilance was necessary still. And for all this effort, "in more than 99 per cent of the cases, the end result of the inquiry was a BIG zero," according to Inspector Norton.

Among the agencies involved with the government's security plan were Customs and Immigration. They took their cue from the government, which announced that visitors' visas would not be given to Iraqis and Palestinians. The agencies made it clear that visitors from the Middle East could expect extra scrutiny. What they did not mention was that all one needed to have was an Arab or Muslim name to face this extraordinary scrutiny.

Syrian-born twenty-five-year-old Wail is a used car dealer in Toronto who imports old cars from the United States. On February 10, he was crossing into Windsor, Ontario, from Detroit at about 9 A.M. At the Customs checkpoint, an officer asked him his nationality, and when he said, "Canadian," he was asked where he was born. He replied that he was born in Syria. Then, the officers wanted to know about the car, and he said it belonged to an American friend who was waiting just past the checkpoint and would take it back with him. He was then asked if he had anything to declare, and he gave them a list of merchandise he had purchased. He was asked to pull over and step away from the car after opening its trunk. Several officers began going through the vehicle with a fine-tooth comb. He protested when one of them, a female officer, began reading his personal diary, in which she also found his passport and his Ontario driver's licence. She told him she could read what she wanted. Another officer examined his passport and questioned him about two visas to Jordan that he had, only one of which he had used. Another officer questioned him about a business card he had listing a business in Detroit. He said he had planned to open a business there with his friend, but the plans fell through. Wail said they then accused him of illegally working in the United States and said if that were true, his Canadian citizenship would be taken away. More than two hours had now passed, and Wail lost his patience. "You can't do a stupid thing like that; it's not possible," he said. The man insisted they could and retorted, according to Wail: "Where have you decided to live: in your country, in Canada or the U.S.?" Wail replied, "What do you mean — my country? This is my country. I am a Canadian." He said the Customs officer replied, "That's not my mistake." Wail was furious.

Eventually, they put him in detention while they searched the car and processed his case. They questioned him about another car he had bought in Detroit, for which he was carrying the ownership papers. He said he would declare it as soon as he imported it into Canada. Having exhausted every avenue, they eventually refused to let him enter on the grounds that he was driving a U.S. car and would have to take it back.

Wail said that, meanwhile, the American who owned the car was standing outside the Customs office. And when Wail said, "Here is the man who owns the car; he'll take it back," the friend stepped in and produced the ownership for the car and his American identification. Customs refused and told him to back off. They said Wail could not drive the car in and only he could take it back. Under the escort of two Customs vehicles, the two drove back to the American side. Wail decided he did not have to take this from his own country and came back saying he would not leave because he was a Canadian: Canada was his country. Wail says that a supervisor threatened to have the car towed to the U.S. side, and his friend convinced him to drive back again.

At the American checkpoint, he was taken to an office. The curious American officer asked him, "Why won't they let you in?" Wail replied that it was because he was driving a U.S. car. "You mean they won't let one of their own citizens in?" the U.S. officer asked. "That's strange." In fifteen minutes, they sent him back to the Canadian side, much to the surprise of the Canada Customs officer who apparently expected U.S. Customs to hold him. This time, his friend was driving. Wail said the same officers came over smiling and laughing and said they had just been doing their job. For Wail, it was no laughing matter. When he finally entered Canada it was almost 3 P.M. — a full five and a half hours had elapsed.

He found it ironic that the inside cover of his Canadian passport has a message for other governments, requesting them to "allow the bearer to pass freely without let or hindrance and to afford the bearer such assistance and protection as may be necessary." Said Wail, "Do they really expect others to allow Canadians to pass freely when they don't do it themselves?"

The powers that the security forces were allowed to exercise during the Gulf War were extremely broad. The targeting of individuals was a violation of the Charter of Rights and Freedoms, which prohibits discrimination based on race, religion, and national origin. Not only did the two agencies violate civil rights, but also they managed to stifle dissent and free expression of belief. Many Arabs and Muslims did not attend demonstrations or any other meetings because they were afraid of being photo-graphed and put under surveillance. In Mississauga, for example, the Muslim community had organized a fund-raising dinner for a centre it is building. It sold out all two hundred tickets. Only seventy people showed up.

The government, meanwhile, in a deliberate and irresponsible act, did not publicize the CSIS assessments that showed little risk of terrorism in Canada. Even a step such as this would have persuaded the non-Arab and non-Muslim population to view the minority group in a kinder light.

Instead, it sought to further its agenda of drumming up support for the war by continuing to play up the bogey of terrorism, although it had little chance of taking place in Canada. In addition, it unleashed the full force of the RCMP through the national emergency plan, not just overreacting, but overreacting to a non-existent threat and that too in a racist manner. The signals that Ottawa sent out spread far and wide, affecting agencies such as Customs and Immigration, which began obstructing and humiliating not just suspected foreigners but even long-time Canadian citizens. If the idea of multiculturalism is to make new Canadians feel at home in the country and to help integrate them, the calendar had been set back by many, many years.

CHAPTER ELEVEN

Making the News

"Nomad is a treacherous desert warrior. He is as unstable as the blowing desert sands, as cold as the desert nights, and as dangerous as the deadly desert scorpion. His only family is a wandering band of cutthroats and thieves. They are men without honor, who use their knowledge of the desert to carry out terrorist assaults on innocent villages."

Description of an Arab doll marketed by Coleco
as part of the Enemies of Rambo series

The Canadian media did not have to make news during the Gulf War. It was made for them by the Pentagon, by the smart bombs and laser-guided bombs, by night-vision goggles and Bouncing Betty bombs that explode at waist level to cut a human in half, and by the cleverly timed release of censored information and television clips. Where the media needed to be creative was in manufacturing the local angle — injecting excitement on the home front.

Historically, Arabs and Muslims have been stereotyped in the Western media, and this bias continued during coverage of the Gulf War, even among the new buzzwords popularized by the U.S. military. The large-scale deaths and injuries among Iraqi civilians, for instance, were called "collateral damage" to soften their impact on the home front. *Time* magazine defined this linguistic coinage as "a term meaning dead or wounded civilians who should have picked a safer neighborhood." Much of the media approached the Gulf War in the same spirit as the Second

World War. It was not unusual to find the coalition forces being referred to as the Allies, the term used in the Second World War, with headlines such as: "Allies Bomb Baghdad" — the image conveyed being one of the Allies battling Adolf Hitler and the Nazis. In fact, the media incessantly compared Saddam Hussein to Hitler and, by extrapolation, the Iraqis and the Arabs who supported Iraq, to the Germans.

Then, there was the mythical threat of Arab and Muslim terrorism in Canada, which became an unquestioned reality in the media. Some dissenting points of view were published, mostly on the Op-Ed pages of the newspapers. These opinions were called the "Arab and Muslim point of view" versus, one supposes, the mainstream point of view. But these articles were few, and whatever redeeming value they may have had was washed away in the euphoria with which the media described the superiority of the white world's war technology.

The media's treatment of Arabs and Muslims in the past is worthy of an entire book in itself, but one news story that played out for weeks all the across the country is worth noting. It did more damage than any other to the Arab image in Canada. It was published in the *Globe and Mail,* Canada's "national newspaper," in 1975, as a copyright story based on a purported leak from the RCMP.

Montreal was hosting the 1976 Olympics, and the *Globe* claimed that the Mounties had uncovered a conspiracy by fourteen Canadian Arabs to commit terrorism at the Games but did not have enough proof to lay charges. As proof, the paper talked of conspiratorial meetings of Arabs at two Middle Eastern restaurants in Windsor, Ontario, and at "another ethnic restaurant" nearby, where the scheme was being drawn up. It said the plot was being hatched in Edmonton, Windsor, Toronto, Montreal, London, Brantford, and other cities. The cities named were those where executive members of the Arab Federation resided.

A paragraph that made little sense read: "The sources said that the suspected conspirators know the police are aware of their planning, but this does not appear to make them any the less dangerous. They are willing, able and in positions to provide food, accommodation, transportation, weapons, intelligence ... for Arab or other terrorists."

Everyone from the justice minister to the RCMP commissioner denied the story, which was picked up by every newspaper and TV and radio station across the country. This was the first time Canada had hosted the Olympics. It was big news. And the story was not received kindly by the Canadian population.

Warren Almand, who was the solicitor general in the Liberal government, accused the *Globe* of acting as an agent for anti-Arab groups. In communities with small Arab populations, local Arabs were being asked to respond and being put on the spot. Ramzi Twal wanted to comment in the local newspaper, the Brantford *Expositor*. He was a well-known local Arab in that small Ontario town, and his co-workers at the Massey-Ferguson factory had begun kidding him that maybe he was one of the fourteen terrorists. The paper made him sign a declaration that he would not sue the *Expositor* before it would publish his comments. All he wanted to say was that the *Globe* story was "pure racism and trash."

The Arab community sued, but there was little provision in Canadian law to launch a class action suit. Eventually, after they had spent about $10,000, they dropped the suit, and the incident was relinquished to Canadian-Arab folklore, as yet another example of media bias.

Although much had changed by the time the Gulf War began — the media had finally recognized the legitimate rights of the Palestinians and the Arabs, and it is unlikely the *Globe* would have published the same story today — old attitudes die hard. And besides, minorities generally are so grossly underrepresented in the Canadian media that any question of sensitivity in the war coverage would be left to the largesse of white editors. A 1988 study done by a McMaster University student showed that visible minorities, native peoples, and the disabled made up 1.7 per cent of staff in newsrooms of papers that represented a third of the total daily newspaper circulation in Canada.

In addition, there was the question of competition and daily deadlines — beating the opposition even if this meant running with half-baked stories. Hence, when the media began looking for domestic villains and started writing stories about an internal threat, the security forces deliberately allowed them to go on a feeding frenzy without any responsible commentary to tone down a line of stories that they knew were false. After all, the more paranoia that was generated, the more it would justify the actions of the security forces.

Subsequently, the media coverage took on a life of its own, and it became a question of who was feeding whom. At one stage, according to Inspector Robert Norton of the RCMP, commander of the force's national wartime operations, the police were actually taking leads from the media to answer their bosses, who were facing questions from the cabinet every time a domestic terrorism story surfaced. It became a cesspool in which everybody was feeding off everybody else at the expense of the Arabs and Muslims.

The paper that led the way in writing about domestic terrorism was the popular Toronto tabloid, the *Sun*. The *Sun* has a history of supporting right-wing causes and taking extreme viewpoints. Peace demonstrations before the war began were dismissed by the paper as the work of naive fools. With the war looming, the *Sun* decided to go looking for terrorists. On January 6, ten days before the United States began bombing Baghdad, the *Sun* published a copyright story that the Federal Bureau of Investigation in the United States had identified twelve pro-Iraqi agents in Metro Toronto who were plotting disruptions in case a war started.

It quoted an FBI spokesman named Mike Garish as saying that the bureau had found out that there were a hundred such agents in North America, with twelve of them in Toronto. "These people are a real big threat that have to be taken very seriously. There is a very high level security problem up there [in Toronto]," Garish was quoted as saying. He refused to identify the potential terrorist targets the agents might aim for in the Toronto area, but he said the FBI had launched a joint operation with the RCMP to round them up.

On January 7, the paper followed up with reactions from Maurice Tugwell of the Mackenzie Institute, a right-wing conflict studies think-tank in Toronto. It quoted him as saying that the FBI numbers are "a credible estimate" and that Canada should follow Britain's example by expelling Iraqi diplomats and interning Iraqis suspected of subversive activities. Another expert on terrorism said he wouldn't be surprised to see one or two terrorist incidents in Canada.

On day three, the *Sun* ran a headline on page two that read: "Police Task Force Targets Agents of Terror." The story said that the Metro Toronto Police and the RCMP had set up a task force to prevent terrorism in the city. It quoted Metro Inspector Jim Neish of the intelligence unit as saying: "You can look at any spot in Metro Toronto to be a target. There are many places where a terrorist could attack to make their point known."

On January 9, the *Sun* said Ontario Hydro had beefed up anti-terrorist security at all its installations, especially the nuclear power plants at Darlington, Pickering (where Abdullah Massih Thomas worked), and Bruce, as a result of the FBI alert. On January 10, major Canadian airports, it said, were staging mock emergency drills in preparation for terrorist attacks, thanks to the FBI warning. After a day of rest, when the *Globe* ran a large Canadian Press story on the terrorist threat from radical Arab and Palestinian groups, the *Sun* reported on January 13 that the Metro Toronto Police had identified possible targets that terrorists could hit. On January 16, when the bombing started, the *Sun* had a story about a terrorism alert across the country, with special centres set up by the RCMP. In the same story, it said the Canadian Arab Federation was bracing for imminent racism against Arabs in Canada. Given all the damaging publicity that the media had created for the community, CAF's reaction was not surprising. And the day after the war began, the *Sun* said that security had in fact been tightened all over the country to prevent possible terrorist attacks from Iraqis and from pro-Palestinian groups. It said Solicitor General Pierre Cadieux was taking the terrorism threat "very seriously."

The *Sun* stories were picked up by the media across the country and distributed by the Canadian Press news agency, as was the 1975 *Globe* story on the terrorism plot regarding the Olympics. The stories also started off what is known in the media as a matching game, as the *Globe* and the Toronto *Star* jumped in to find their own terrorist networks. Print and broadcast outlets across Canada in the larger cities undertook similar missions, hoping, one supposes, to find local Arab and Muslim terrorists. Neither could match the *Sun*'s special on the dirty dozen. A *Star* editor said that its reporters even checked the FBI personnel records and could come up with no employee called Mike Garish. There may have been good reason for that as the RCMP, which also heard about the dirty dozen from the *Sun*, found out.

Inspector Robert Norton was in charge of the Ottawa-based National Emergency Operations Centre. He was instrumental in putting together the strategic plan that was implemented once the war started, and he remembers the *Sun* story very clearly. "Oh that one," he said in an interview. "We tracked the *Sun* story. The reporter phoned FBI headquarters and interviewed the person who answered the phone. The man quoted in the story did not exist in the FBI. He was with an accounting firm. It was he who gave the reporter some type of a story. The [freelance] accountant did admit [to the RCMP and FBI] that he gave the reporter that story. There was nothing to it."

The *Sun*, however, insisted its story was accurate. In its follow-up story on January 8, it wrote that the FBI had confirmed that the *Sun* "had spoken" with the bureau, "amid reports that Garish was not a spokesman for the Bureau." Les Pyette, the *Sun*'s executive editor, is quoted in the story as saying: "We stand by our story. Someone at the FBI number in Washington spoke at length on the Iraqi issue with our reporter."

The argument was ludicrous at best. The voice at the other end may well have been the FBI's janitor instead of a freelance accountant who happened to be near the telephone. But Pyette said in an interview that the *Sun* did try to find out the truth after the story was questioned by the other media. He said the reporter, Tom Godfrey, who is considered a hard-working journalist, and Pyette himself kept "bugging the FBI and the RCMP" to tell the paper if the story was wrong so that the *Sun* could correct it. "The RCMP should have called and told me, and we would have fixed it, but nobody did." He said about seven to ten days later, the FBI faxed him a letter saying that there was no such person on staff. Pyette said by then the incident had gone so far in terms of follow-ups that he angrily threw the letter in the garbage.

His version of the events is that Godfrey called the FBI on the weekend and was transferred to either the home or the office of the weekend spokesperson, who turned out to be Mike Garish. He said Garish spoke to Godfrey for about fifteen minutes. "Later on this Mike Garish disappears. He's nowhere to be found. Godfrey is a good reporter, I know he talked to him, I examined all his notes. But, after the story appeared, I guess the FBI figured he should not have talked and Garish disappears. You know how these intelligence types are. I don't trust them, either in Canada or outside."

The RCMP never did make the contents of its finding on Garish public, except to the executive level of the government, which was fielding questions from the cabinet. It left it to the FBI, since it was that agency's case to begin with. The Canadian government also decided to keep mum rather than dampen a paranoia that was working to its advantage on the home front, with the Arabs and Muslims as its enemy.

On January 18, two days after the war started, the *Globe* had its own terrorism story, saying that although Canada was at low risk, security had been stepped up. It repeated much of the information the *Sun* had carried earlier, except for a bomb threat at a large shopping centre in Toronto, presumably the Eaton's Centre. The media usually do not report bomb threats — the police receive scores of them every month — because the feeling is that the publicity only encourages more pranksters. The *Globe* quoted Alan Bell of Intercon Security as saying that the mall was on a high state of terrorism alert as a result of the threat, which may well have been the work of anti-Arab and anti-Muslim pranksters.

Not about to be outdone, the Toronto *Star* reported on January 21 that the prime minister believed that there was a real threat of Iraqi terrorist attacks in Canada — perhaps Brian Mulroney had not been reading the reports from CSIS. In the next paragraph the *Star* said that according to Solicitor General Pierre Cadieux the threat was "not imminent." It then reiterated a story floated by an American TV network, which the RCMP would find to be false, about terrorists headed to the United States via Canada. The *Star* went on to report a plea from the Canadian Arab Federation asking Canadians not to become paranoid, and then it quoted a University of Toronto professor as saying that "it would be foolish" to discount Arab Canadians as security threats. All of this was crammed into one story in which the *Star* tried to compete with the other two papers while still maintaining some level of sensitivity towards the Arabs and Muslims.

There was yet another incident on January 25 that all the media, with the exception of the *Star*, jumped on and quickly connected to the war and terrorism. An eighteen-year-old high school student named Haruki Ahmura was arrested on University Avenue, about a block and a half away from the U.S. consulate. At his home, police found several hand grenades. Police charged him with threatening to bomb the Toronto office of the RCMP. In the morning edition of the Toronto *Star* story, there is no mention of the consulate or of terrorism. In a carefully crafted story that gave its readers the news with sensitivity for the Arab community, it did mention that the man was wearing a small Palestinian flag on his chest. However, the *Star* quickly quoted Police Chief William McCormack as insisting that the public was never in danger and that the flag had nothing to do with the investigation. The *Globe* had a headline that read: "Man Charged after Grenades Found," and below it, a subhead: "Security Tightened at Government Offices around Metro." It claimed, after attending the same press conference that the *Star* attended with McCormack, that the chief would not comment on whether the arrest related to an anti-terrorist investigation or on the significance of the flag. Its story went on to say that neither the RCMP nor CSIS would comment on the case, that the Mounties were investigating all potential terrorism leads, and that security was being tightened at government plants and offices in Toronto because "of a threat of terrorist attacks in Canada during the Persian Gulf War." The *Sun* connected the story immediately to the threat of terrorism that it had been warning its readers about.

On April 9, the man pleaded guilty and was jailed for fifteen months, put on three years probation, and ordered to continue with psychiatric treatment. This was his second arrest on similar charges. In reporting the sentence, the *Sun* repeated its earlier interview with Ahmura's housemate, who said that the man was sympathetic to Arab causes — implying a sinister underside to the whole case that even the police had discounted.

Inspector Norton said while the media again immediately connected this incident to the war, it had nothing to do with the terrorism alert. "The arrest just happened to take place near the consulate, and so the media just assumed there was a connection. It wasn't even our case; it was a local case," he said. The RCMP has a policy of not commenting on another force's case, and so it did not make a public statement that Ahmura was not an Arab terrorist let loose on the streets of Toronto. In fact, he was part Japanese.

The RCMP's National Emergency Operations Centre had a special unit to monitor all the newscasts and was again caught by surprise, this time on the weekend of January 19. ABC, an American TV network, reported in a live interview with its reporter from Scandinavia that Iraqi terrorists were heading to Canada en route to the United States to commit acts of terrorism. NEOC knew that the next morning, as in the case of the *Sun*'s story, it would have to respond to questions from cabinet. "That story too grew like a snowball," Inspector Norton said, referring to news stories about the network's claim in all major Canadian papers and on TV and radio stations. "Where he [the ABC reporter] got the story from, we don't know. But it was totally, totally false from our point of view."

The result of all this reporting was paranoia. Sporting goods stores began selling gas masks as they had never done before; citizens began to fear Saddam Hussein's terrorists would explode chemical weapons in Toronto. In the Scarborough suburb of Toronto, which is adjacent to Pickering, the site of Ontario Hydro's nuclear reactor, the school board drew up evacuation plans. It sent letters about this plan to parents, creating near hysteria. Schools in the area began buying out anti-radiation potassium iodine pills in case terrorists struck at the reactor. Jerry's Drug Warehouse stores in Pickering, Whitby, and Scarborough sold five hundred bottles of such pills in one day.

Also delighted with such reporting were private security firms, as they swung into action with security systems that cost anywhere from $200,000 to more than $1 million. What could be better for business than to have the lead paragraph of a story in the prestigious Report on Business section of the *Globe* say, "Since Iraqi president Saddam Hussein's call for Muslims to strike at his enemies, wherever they may be, the potential targets — businesses and individuals — have turned to private security consultants in unprecedented numbers." Or for its tabloid competitor, the *Financial Post,* to describe how one such consultant could not get through to his office on the telephone because potential clients were jamming the lines and then to quote another consultant with these ominous words: "Canada's large undefended border may prove tempting for terrorists unable to get into U.S. cities. ... As an important financial and political centre, Toronto could be attacked by groups unable to get to Chicago or New York."

Were any of the media concerned about what was happening at the receiving end of all this reporting? The paper that has historically led the way in reporting minority points of view is the Toronto *Star*. During the Depression, when the Toronto police had taken it upon themselves to wipe out the Communist Party and would raid its offices without warrants, confiscate its books and documents, and charge its peaceful rallies with horses, it was the *Star* that spoke up for dissent and the freedom of assembly and speech.

Once again, during the Gulf War, the *Star* supported the rights of the underdog. It ran several stories about the concerns in the Arab and Muslim communities. Several of these stories were put on the front page, including one that detailed racism in schools and workplaces and examined the CSIS and RCMP interviews. This item was followed by a story on the "Journal," a popular current affairs TV show produced by the Canadian Broadcasting Corporation, on the same topic.

However, not everyone at the *Star* agreed with the points of view expressed in these articles. In Rosie DiManno's column, the writing harked back to the days when Arabs were always suspect and the police were doing the right thing in investigating the community. After the first Iraqi Scud missiles had landed in Tel Aviv and three people had died of heart attacks, DiManno's column was about a sombre synagogue service, where Immigration Minister Barbara McDougall shed tears as the congregation prayed for the safety of Israel — at a time when the combined power of the bombs dropped on Baghdad had surpassed those of the atomic bombs dropped on Hiroshima and Nagasaki. Then DiManno followed up with columns questioning the political agendas of the pacifists and Muslims. And finally, when the issue of CSIS interrogations surfaced, she wrote: "If we do have an agency called CSIS, and it does have a government mandate to do a certain job, can it be criticized for doing that job, especially in what appears to be such a reticent, cautious and almost comically obvious manner? And particularly when Saddam Hussein has issued repeated threats of international terrorism. When he has also called up Muslims around the world to participate in what he insists on describing as a Holy War."

The interrogations may have been comical for DiManno, but Arabs and Muslims weren't laughing. One wonders if it occurred to her that in a democracy security forces should not be unleashed to interrogate hundreds of citizens and that responsible politicians do not paint an entire community with a broad brush. And if DiManno was not aware of what was happening to these communities, surely as a reporter and columnist it was her job to find out before she dismissed Arab and Muslim complaints.

Other columnists, such as William Johnson of Montreal's English-language daily, the *Gazette,* also engaged in Arab and Muslim bashing. He displayed a truly amazing re-creation of the white man's burden in a column that could have come out of England in the 1890s:

> The true war objectives now, though never previously acknowledged explicitly, are on a scale that justified all the deaths and destruction occasioned by the war. ...
>
> It is now essential that Saddam be removed from power. And the war machine he has constructed over so many years must be destroyed. These are the premises of the new war aims. Only thus can an attack on Israel a few years hence be prevented.
>
> The feudal structures of the Middle East, whether in the form of emirates and kingdoms, or Iranian theocracies, or ambitious barons like Saddam Hussein, are all condemned. The modern world requires democracy, religious and cultural pluralism, the rule of law and the sharing of wealth. The countries where Islam is the religion of the people must learn to adapt to the modern world or pay a terrible price.

By modern, of course, Johnson meant Western. Whatever his motives, his article made the bulletin boards of the local mosques as an example of the kind of bias Muslims must face. Although the few stories published by the *Star* and carried on the "Journal" documentary were heroic efforts to report on persecution at home, what was needed was not heroic efforts but a crusade to force authorities to stop putting the Arabs and Muslims under siege with intimidating tactics. But, as the authorities had gambled, the media were too busy to get involved in such investigative reporting.

The news treatment only served to reinforce the Arab and Muslim feeling that there was a double standard in reporting. At home, the Canadian media clearly missed the biggest war story — the persecution of Arabs and Muslims by the government and the extreme racism its policies fostered. There were scores of lapses in Canada's war policies and aims and in its domestic security operation, but where was the investigative reporting? When some Arabs tried to make a public issue of the intolerance and racial harassment that they had encountered, the media demanded more proof — their word as Canadians was not enough. The implicit allegation in this media response was that the communities were just making up fairy tales.

Politics in the Middle East are complex, and violence is deep rooted, often originating as a result of the colonization of the region by Western powers. And yet, during the Gulf War, the media took their cue from Washington and Ottawa. Instead of maintaining an independent, critical, and fair-minded approach, they copied the cheerleading role of the American media just as Brian Mulroney's government copied the policies of its counterpart in the United States. This uncritical presentation of the events of the war was bound to create a gulf within Canada itself. And when it did, and Arabs and Muslims were subjected to racial intolerance, this reaction was either glossed over by the media or ignored. Leads provided by Canadian Arabs that could have led to news stories about racism were considered suspect. Their offers to put the conflict into perspective were rejected. Balance and fairness — those traditional pillars of journalism — were largely missing from its information package. And the question of educating the public, in addition to simply informing it, remained unfulfilled.

In journalism, one of the driving forces is reflected in an oft-repeated and romantic credo: "Comforting the afflicted and afflicting the comfortable." During the Gulf War, the Canadian media turned this credo on its head. Their reporting would comfort the comfortable, and their omissions would afflict the afflicted.

CHAPTER TWELVE

The Crumbling Mosaic

"We have all these multiculturalism policies put up on our walls and then we go and join the forces of America. ... I think if Canada had the guts, it would have said we will stand neutral and offer medical and other aid. Then they would have been looked up to. Some friends of mine are ashamed to wear the Canadian flag to Europe. Now when people see the Maple Leaf, they are seeing the Stars and Stripes forever."

Laura van der Smissen, race relations officer, Dufferin-Peel Roman Catholic School Board, and ethnic historian

Within weeks after the end of the Gulf War, it had become a distant memory — preserved on video clips in network archives, awaiting a documentary filmmaker. For Ottawa, the short, devastating, and one-sided battle had achieved all its objectives — Kuwait had been liberated, at least for its monarch, and freedom and democracy had been restored in a land where the emir did not tolerate any criticism. For the politicians, there was no need to discuss it any more.

But there were others who did not want to forget or forgive that easily. And not all of them were Arabs and Muslims who had suffered during the conflict. There were those who had bought into Canada's ideals of multiculturalism and its image as the peacemaker of the world. As they watched the massacre of more than a hundred thousand Iraqis in the Middle East and the persecution of Arabs and Muslims in Canada, they began to raise some interesting questions. Foremost among them: Was multicul-

turalism simply a selling job? Was it just lip service paid to lofty
ideals? Or did multiculturalism bring with it the need for Canada
to consider the damaging effects within the country of getting
militarily involved in foreign conflicts? As the Gulf War shows,
there is a tremendous potential for long-term damage to Canada's
social fabric and for fanning the flames of racism, hatred, and
intolerance.

To begin with, what is multiculturalism and what does it have
to do with the Gulf conflict? Historically, there are two interpreta-
tions of multiculturalism. From the 1960s, immigrants from Third
World countries streamed into Canada, to the point where the
1986 census found that more than 1.6 million of Canada's 26
million population comprises visible minorities, and this figure
excludes native peoples. The 1991 Census is expected to show
visible minorities alone at more than two million. In addition, if
one lumps together all Canadians whose heritage is neither British
nor French, they number about 38 per cent, a figure that is expected to reach 50 per cent in a few years.

Multiculturalism became official Canadian policy as part of the
Trudeau government's response to the challenge of Quebec. The
Trudeau policy to counter demands for Quebec sovereignty was
bilingualism and multiculturalism for all of Canada. Multiculturalism went several steps further than the American model of the
melting pot, where all newcomers were blended together — a
cultural imperialism of sorts. Canada decided to support immigrants in maintaining their culture.

Cynics, however, labelled the concept a ploy by the Liberal
government of Pierre Trudeau, which saw the ethnics as a massive
vote bank that needed to be nurtured so that voting Liberal became
a family tradition. When Brian Mulroney and the Tories assumed
power in September, 1984, they were no different. They decided
to take multiculturalism several steps further and not only passed
the Canadian Multiculturalism Act, but also set up a separate
department for multiculturalism. If Pierre Trudeau would be remembered for expounding on the multicultural mosaic, the Tories
figured they should be remembered for enshrining it in law.

Laura van der Smissen, the race relations officer with the
Dufferin-Peel Roman Catholic school board just outside Toronto,
is a strong supporter of a multicultural Canada. However, she
believes that as multiculturalism is practised in the country, it only

covers up Canada's continuing racist immigration policy. "His-torically, immigration in Canada is, 'Who do we need now and what do we need them for?' The Chinese built the railroad, and the Italians built the sewers. Now they need the Orientals [Hong Kong Chinese] for their money and their business. I mean they are amazing; they still haven't changed. And next week it will be another group we need; we need neurosurgeons, and they'll find them. ... People have become a commodity. That disturbs me as a parent and educator."

The most curious aspect of the Multiculturalism Act is that it does not define multiculturalism; it simply enshrines the ideals of Canada as a mosaic as verbalized by prime ministers since the time of John Diefenbaker. It is also legislation that has no effect when something as major as the Gulf conflict comes along and the policy of the government in power takes precedence over ethnic minorities.

For instance, it is meant to apply to all federal government departments, crown corporations, agencies, boards, and councils. Section 3 (1) reads: "It is hereby declared to be the policy of the Government of Canada to ... recognize and promote the under-standing that multiculturalism ... provides an invaluable resource in the shaping of Canada's future. ... promote policies, programs and practices that enhance the ability of individuals and communi-ties of all origins to contribute to the continuing evolution of Canada." A government interpretation with the act specifies that these policies must be such that they "respond to the needs of all Canadians" and help them participate fully. It orders the govern-ment to build bridges to these communities and consider their views when developing policies and programmes.

However, Canada did not consider the views of its large Arab and Muslim communities before it decided to join the U.S.-spon-sored coalition in the Gulf. In fact, there wasn't even a full parlia-mentary debate before this decision, let alone the seeking of a consensus from the people. Larry Shaben, a loyal Tory from Edmonton, a former provincial cabinet minister, and a Canadian of Arab descent, and Alan Redway, the federal housing minister, both asked Ottawa to form a consultative group of Arabs before developing a Middle East policy. Shaben's idea was accepted only after the war had ended, but its status is uncertain. Canada's Gulf policy did not help Arabs and Muslims participate fully, nor did it take their needs into account.

Redway realized the need for such a consultative committee even before the act was passed, when, as a Tory back-bencher in the Commons, he was on the standing committee on multiculturalism. He remembers Ukrainians coming before the committee and pointing out their concerns about Canada's foreign policy toward the Soviet Union. They also pointed out that people from all over the world had settled in Canada but that their views were never reflected in Canadian foreign policy. The government did try briefly to consult with Chinese Canadians after the student uprising and the killings at Beijing's Tiananmen Square. A group of Chinese Canadians was formed to advise the government and to listen to the government rationale for the policy it was adopting. The government hoped these views would then be communicated to the Canadian-Chinese population. However, soon after the incident in China, Ottawa fell in line with Washington, trade relations with China were normalized, and the consultation became a farce.

Redway said the message the Ukrainians brought registered on him after the committee hearings. "Since then I felt that we could be using their background and knowledge to a much greater extent. There is a pent up frustration in these communities because we have a very professional foreign service which has developed a tradition of its own. In a sense it is [sacred]."

In a heated conversation with Joe Clark at a Tory policy convention during the war, Shaben blasted him for joining the war, pointing out that the foreign policy misadventure being embarked upon was clearly not driven by the national needs of Canada and its people. His criticism fell on deaf ears. Ottawa had already made up its mind to join in Washington's war.

Having done that, however, could the Arabs and Muslims have used the Multiculturalism Act to force a consultative approach in place of policy-making in a vacuum? Hardly. If the act does not define multiculturalism, it also has no enforcement mechanism — the government had even turned down a language commissioner who could monitor one of its provisions, promoting the native tongues of new Canadians. And statutes, says Professor Harish Jain of McMaster University, cannot govern themselves. Jain believes that laudable as the act is, it has turned out to be fairly exclusionary for people of colour and races other than European. The bottom line of multiculturalism has become what Jain calls "cultural dollars" — we'll pay for you to keep your songs and dances and costumes, but we choose to neglect your involvement in social policy.

During the Gulf conflict some critics began thinking about solutions to what had occurred in that tumultuous period within the confines of Canada. Among them was Tad Mitsui, a minister of the United Church of Canada. He is also the associate secretary of the justice and peace committee of the Canadian Council of Churches, a group that strongly denounced Canada's support of and involvement in the Gulf War. Mitsui grew up in Japan when it was being bombed by America during the Second World War. During the Korean War, when America forced Japan to arm itself, he came down on the side of pacifism, demonstrating against weaponry and speaking out for peace.

After joining the church, he spent several years in Africa, the Middle East, and Europe, before deliberately picking Canada because of its multiculturalism — he found the American melting pot concept unacceptable. But it was the six years that he spent in Switzerland that shaped his views on neutrality. And the Gulf War, with the persecution of Arabs and Muslims in Canada, synthesized his views on neutrality in the Canadian context.

He said: "There is race involved in judging who is an enemy and who is a friend. For example, Canadians will never think of America as an enemy, and neither can they think of the British or the French as enemies, and nowadays even Germany. But it is so easy for Canadians to think of Arabs as the enemy. On the other hand, they will never think of Israelis as the enemy. And if you start to classify the subconscious psyche of Canadians — who can and who cannot be the enemy — it so turns out that most of the countries with which Canada cannot engage in war are white ... and so it cannot be wrong to advocate their policy. I think this is not fair. Why can't Pakistan be our friend no matter what? Why can't Iraq, to take the case to its extreme, be our friend? Israel is one of the world's worst culprits in terms of human rights violations and yet nobody, nobody will think of Israel as an enemy. And so there is nothing wrong with the policies of the Israeli government. And if you expand that logic, if Canada should exist as a multicultural, multiracial country, you cannot take sides with anybody."

Since multiculturalism advocates celebrating the differences, allowing the cultures and traditions to co-exist, the extension of that policy in foreign policy is a stance of neutrality. He believes that the full implication of multiculturalism, in fact, is neutrality and the abandonment of all the assumptions about who can and cannot be Canada's enemy. This does not mean that Canada should remain silent on the world stage. It can still criticize and take a stand at the United Nations. It can play an active role, as we have many times, as a peacekeeper. But it should draw a line when someone like U.S. President George Bush comes along and requests that Canada participate in an offensive war.

Mitsui has an interesting analogy that stretches the assumptions of white Canadian thinking to its extreme. What if Britain, France, and Israel restaged the 1953 invasion of Egypt's Suez Canal today? Given the white-dominated thinking, Canada would never advocate turning its guns against Britain. None of the three can be construed under present Canadian policy as enemies, even though they clearly would be the invaders under any standard of international law, much as Iraq was the invader in the Gulf conflict. Clearly, the situation would raise a double standard. And what about Egyptian Canadians? What would they do? In an ideal, multicultural society, they should be allowed to advocate turning the guns against Britain, since it was the invader. But would they be able to do this without fear of being subjected to what the Arabs and Muslims went through in the Gulf conflict? It would again become a case of forcing Egyptian Canadians to divide their loyalties and live in fear.

Culture, Mitsui argues, is very often connected to people's sense of identity, and it is cruel to force them to divide their loyalties or deny their loyalty to their motherland. He believes it damages the psyche when people are forced to separate themselves from their cultural identity, which is often linked to what is happening in the old country. Given this fact, Mitsui applauded a University of Toronto professor, an Iraqi, when she bluntly told a radio interviewer during the war that she hoped Saddam Hussein would win. He had seen enough other Arab Canadians hide their views.

"My ideal society, if we continue to have a multiracial society where cultures co-exist, is one where anybody is allowed to say anything like that, which can otherwise sound almost taboo. ... I lived in Switzerland for six years. It is a very well-controlled country, it is heavily armed for defensive purposes and has retaliation capability, but, on the other hand, because of its neutrality, everybody is allowed to say anything, and nobody is scandalized."

Mitsui, like Jain and others, believes that although neutrality would not be a panacea for all the racism that continues unabated in Canada, in the case of the Gulf War it would have dampened the backlash suffered by Arabs and Muslims. The fear among people such as Mitsui is that today it is Iraqis, tomorrow it could be any of the other nationalities settled here, if Ottawa continues to fall behind Washington in the American quest for a post-Cold War "New World Order."

Larry Shaben tried to put this concept of neutrality forward at a policy convention of the Tories in Edmonton, reminding his fellow Conservatives of the peacekeeping role that Canada had embarked upon. He recalls being sharply rebutted and reminded that traditionally Canada was not a neutral country, given its role in the First and Second World Wars and the Korean War and its membership in the North Atlantic Treaty Organization (NATO). Saleem Qureshi, a political scientist at the University of Alberta, pointed out that neutral countries such as Switzerland, Sweden, and Austria were historical and traditional societies that had evolved as neutral after centuries of politics. Canada, he said, is a heterogeneous society that is still in the formative stage. Yes, it is possible for Canada to evolve toward neutrality, he said, but it would have to be by a process in which ethnic Canadians played a large part by getting involved in the political system. They would have to make their voices heard, and the government would have to listen to them.

If there is any lesson to be learned from the Gulf conflict for Canada, it is simply this: Time is running out quickly for a country that had promised to show the world how different nationalities can peacefully co-exist under one roof. At the time this book was written, Canada was embroiled in a fractious constitutional debate — French Canada was threatening to separate if it did not get a distinct spot in the mosaic, and the right-wing Reform party of

Preston Manning was moving up in the opinion polls as it advocated an end to multiculturalism. Joe Clark had been moved from External Affairs to Constitutional Affairs to forge a new constitution and a new federal-provincial relationship. Our native peoples, those original inhabitants of Canada whose lands were seized by colonial British and French forces and by successive Canadian governments, have only just managed to assure their place in the forging of this relationship. And they won this place only after an armed stand-off at Oka, outside Montreal, in 1990, in which Ottawa came close to turning its armed forces against people with a just cause.

But where was the non-English, non-French voice in all of this? Where was multiculturalism? Did other ethnic groups not deserve to be part of the debate? All there is now is an ambiguous clause in the existing Charter of Rights and Freedoms that reads that the document "shall be interpreted in a manner consistent with the preservation and enhancement of the multicultural heritage of Canadians." But the way the debate is headed it appears that the two dominant white races in Canada may well push ethnic minorities to the sidelines while they forge a new alliance to keep Canada together. Within the Tories themselves, there is a movement afoot to dismantle the ministry of multiculturalism and do away with it — no doubt a move to counter the growing popularity of the Reform Party, which could eat into Conservative strongholds.

Unless Canada's minorities raise their voices and demand to be included in the debate, they will likely not get a distinct spot of their own in a document that will become the cornerstone of Canadian law.

For an alternative, one can only hark back to the words of Mikha Yakow, the Canadian Iraqi whose son Fares was beaten up by a white gang outside a Toronto school, "I ask Canada and the people of Canada, 'Why do you open your doors to another population to come here, and then you make war on their country and you show hatred to those people here?' "

Why indeed?

SOURCES

In addition to the interviews conducted for this book, the following sources were also consulted:

Print Media:
Now magazine, the *Globe and Mail,* the *Toronto Star,* the *Toronto Sun,* the *Montreal Gazette, La Presse,* the *Hamilton Spectator,* the *London Free Press,* the *Winnipeg Free Press,* the *Edmonton Journal,* the *Edmonton Sun,* the *Vancouver Sun,* the *Financial Post,* the *Markham Economist* and *Sun, Time* magazine, the *Financial Times* of London, the *New York Times,* the *Wall Street Journal,* the Washington *Post,* the LA *Times,* Z magazine, the *Village Voice,* the *Nation, Harper's, Lies of Our Times.*

Books:
Abu-Laban, Baha. *An Olive Branch on the Family Tree: The Arabs in Canada.* Toronto, Ottawa: McClelland & Stewart; Multiculturalism Canada, 1980.

Abu-Laban, Baha, and Faith T. Zeady, eds. *Arabs in America: Myths and Realities.* Wilmette, IL: Medina UP International, 1975.

Berton, Pierre. *The Great Depression.* Toronto: McClelland & Stewart, 1990.

Mortimer, Edward. *Faith and Power: The Politics of Islam.* London: Faber and Faber, 1982.

Said, Edward W. *Covering Islam.* New York: Pantheon, 1981.

Shaheen, Jack G. *The TV Arab.* Bowling Green, OH: Bowling Green State U Popular P, 1984.

Waugh, Earl H., Baha Abu-Laban, and Regula B. Qureshi, eds. *The Muslim Community in North America.* Edmonton: U of Alberta P, 1983.

Other Sources:
Canada. Parliament. House of Commons. Standing Committee on External Affairs and International Trade. *Minutes.* Issues 79–98. Ottawa: Queen's Printer, 1991.

The Canadian Multiculturalism Act.

Canadian Council of Churches. *Position Paper on Middle East.* Toronto: Canadian Council of Churches, 1990.